DURDLE DOOR
TO DARTMOOR

Also available from The Sundial Press

THE BLACKTHORN WINTER by Philippa Powys

HESTER CRADDOCK by Alyse Gregory

DURDLE DOOR
TO DARTMOOR

Wessex Essays

of

LLEWELYN POWYS

Selected and arranged by Anthony Head and Frank Kibblewhite

THE SUNDIAL PRESS
2007

This selection of essays by Llewelyn Powys is taken from the following collections: *Dorset Essays*, *Earth Memories*, *Somerset Essays*, *A Baker's Dozen* and *Wessex Memories*

This edition is published by The Sundial Press

46 The Sheeplands, Sherborne, Dorset DT9 4BS

www.sundialpress.co.uk

Cover design by Frank Kibblewhite

Front cover picture © Nicholas Hely Hutchinson

www.nicholashelyhutchinson.com

ISBN 0-9551523-4-8   ISBN 978-0-9551523-4-4

Printed by Biddles Ltd, Kings Lynn, Norfolk

'Consider the glow, the glory of being alive, the incredible chance of it! How heart-piercing, how shocking, how supremely beautiful is this unexplained, wavering movement that troubles all that is, from the Milky Way to a common sting-nettle!'

Llewelyn Powys

CONTENTS

Foreword

Foreword

Llewelyn Powys (1884-1939) was a member of one of Britain's most remarkable literary families. Born in Dorchester, he was the eighth of the eleven multi-talented children of the Rev. Charles Francis Powys, vicar of Montacute in Somerset, and Mary Cowper Johnson. His brothers included the writers John Cowper Powys and T. F. Powys, as well as Littleton Powys, headmaster of Sherborne Prep. School, and the architect A. R. Powys, both of whom also published several books; while his sisters included the novelist and poet Philippa Powys, the artist Gertrude Powys, and Marian Powys, who became a leading authority on lace and a curator at the Metropolitan Museum of New York. Among his ancestry he could also number the poets John Donne and William Cowper.

Llewelyn spent his childhood in Dorset and Somerset, and returned to the West Country after his university days at Corpus Christi College, Cambridge, to work as a private tutor and school-master. In 1909 he contracted tuberculosis, a disease that was to remain with him and profoundly affect his outlook on life. It took him off immediately to Clavadel Sanatorium in Switzerland in search of a cure, and subsequently to Gilgil in British East Africa, where another of his brothers, William, was farming. The four years he spent there as a stock farm manager opened his eyes to the awful brutality of the natural world and gave him the raw materials for his first ventures into journalism when he moved to America in 1920 to join his brother John Cowper, who was making his living there as an itinerant lecturer.

The rapid popularity of his sketches of African life led to the publication of two collections, *Ebony and Ivory* (1923) and *Black Laughter* (1924), and the quality of his other literary and philosophical essays in various journals also brought him to the attention of the wider literary world in America, where he soon developed close friendships with such luminaries as the novelist Theodore Dreiser and the poet Edna St Vincent Millay. It was also at this time that he met and married Alyse Gregory, then the editor of the pioneering journal *The Dial*, who later became a novelist and essayist in her own right. Llewelyn Powys's other works of the 1920s – among them the autobiographical *Skin for Skin* (1925) and his portrait of contemporary America, *The Verdict of Bridlegoose* (1926) – established his reputation as a writer of rich and vivid prose, while in later philosophical works such as *A Pagan's Pilgrimage* (1931), *Impassioned Clay* (1931) and *Glory of Life* (1934) he developed and propagated the Epicurean philosophy that sustained him through all his tribulations.

But it was in the numerous Wessex essays he wrote when he was finally settled again in his native Dorset, first at the White Nose and then in East Chaldon in an isolated house high up on the cliffs, that Llewelyn Powys proved himself to be one of the great observers and portrayers of country life in England, one who could take his rightful place beside the likes of Gilbert White, W. H. Hudson, William Cobbett, and Richard Jefferies in the pantheon of English rural writers. In *Earth Memories* (1934), *Dorset Essays* (1935) and *Somerset Essays* (1937) he distilled his reverence for Nature with his own deep knowledge of local landscape and history to produce some of his most evocative and memorable essays, casting a bold and compassionate light not only on local characters and incidents but on the long procession of human history beneath the endless unforgiving heavens.

As his health deteriorated he returned to Switzerland, where he completed his strangely beautiful and sensuous novel *Love and Death* not long before his own death in the winter of 1939, as the world plunged into madness.

Never a fashionable writer, in some ways an old-fashioned one, Llewelyn Powys was nonetheless a man who spoke to the future through his pen, never ceasing to reiterate his doctrine of simple values and personal happiness, and showing in his own eloquence and fortitude the way to its achievement for all mortal beings. In a modern world in thrall to vacuous celebrity and conspicuous greed, it is both timely and refreshing to encounter a mind and spirit which places such value on the very miracle of existence.

This new collection, *Durdle Door to Dartmoor*, brings together twenty-six of Llewelyn Powys's finest Wessex essays.

The Durdle Door

HOW individual a feature of the Dorset coast is the great oolite archway situated westward of Lulworth Cove known as the Durdle Door. The Pulpit Rock at Portland Bill and the Old Harry Rock between Studland and Swanage are not more dear to natives of Dorset. The Durdle Door is sometimes called the Barn Door, and the homeliness of this title accords well with its shape, for, viewed either from sea or land, this broken cliff has the simple look that often belongs to the entrances of old out-buildings of agrarian husbandry, entrances wide enough to admit a broad-beamed country wagon burdened high with corn sheafs. The appearance of this rugged, firmly standing portal of the open sea suggests an ancient human building, the weathering it has received differing little from the weathering that has fallen upon the square belfry tower of Sherborne Abbey, upon the vaulted ashlar roof of St Catherine's Chapel at Abbotsbury, or upon the mellowed masonry of such venerable secular habitations as Wolfeton House and Melcombe Bingham.

I recall only once having known the ravens to select the Durdle Door for their February nesting. They reared their brood on its precipitous southern wall that year, their insatiable black chicks incessantly calling for their meat across a mackerel sea. It is a remarkable fact that the celebrated promontory has never been favoured by mating gulls. Are they perhaps aware that it is possible for a daring boy to climb along the whole length of the Durdle

Door, whereas to the westward Bats Head offers innumerable marble white ledges, inaccessible without the aid of ropes?

On a summer's morning the Durdle Door Bay can present a very harmless and tranquil appearance. At intervals curling waves break upon its shingle, waves not high enough to overset a child's toy boat. Samphire, flower of St Peter, that has managed to root itself in the rough interstices of the huge sea gate, seems as naturally placed as are patches of mistletoe upon an apple tree bowed down with age. The sea between the Durdle Door and the Blind Cow Rock suggests, when the sun is shining, the blue transparency of the Mediterranean, reminding a lover of Capri of the water surrounding the grottoes on the southern side of the romantic Neapolitan island. Bathers, however, should be careful. Only strong and experienced swimmers should ever venture through the arch into the open sea, for at certain times of the year dangerous currents may be encountered. My father used always to warn us about this, and in my own time I can remember several visitors being drowned. The safest bathing place is to the east of the Durdle Door in St Oswald's Bay. Here the Man-of-War Rock performs the service of a strong breakwater, and it is a happy sight in August to observe human beings basking like seals upon its slippery expanses, thick-matted with seaweed, subjects of the king who might belong to a blither civilisation than it has been our fortune to know. It is possible, indeed, that Phoenician traders, familiar with the gaiety of classical holidays, may have disported themselves on these very boulders – for does not the great down that towers over it take its name, Tout, from the Phoenician deity, Theut, proving beyond all disputation that this section of the coast was well known to those adventurous traffickers of antiquity? Though from the writings of Tacitus it can be inferred that Caractacus died at Rome, there has always existed a persistent rumour amongst the shepherds and fishermen of the Lulworth district that the barrow so ceremoniously crowning Hamboro Tout marks the true burying place of this famous chieftain. A wayfarer who takes the trouble to climb up to this tumulus will be richly rewarded. Its position affords one of the finest views in south Dorset. It was on the summit of Hamboro Tout that Farmer Diffy built his bonfire for the Jubilee of King George, the most impressive Beltane fire seen on that gala night south of the Frome.

From Nore to Tout
Never a flout,
As foxes are free
In earths by the sea,
Each lass and lad
With love is glad.

Squire and farmer
Plowman, crow starver,
As merry as weasels
In a bed of teasels,
As frolic as stoats
In a field of oats.

THE DURDLE DOOR

Of the world of convention
I pray you no mention,
Tingling with malice
From cottage to palace
It can change overnight
Wrong into right.

I well remember the occasion when I first saw the Durdle Door. We children had come by the Lulworth steamer from Weymouth under the care of our nurse Emily. I could not have been ten years old. Walking up the street from the Cove we stood spellbound by the spectacle of a large cat outside the door of one of the cottages. This cat was being treated as if it were a dog. It had a leather collar about its neck and a chain attached to a kennel. The animal looked so content and well cared for that my sister put out her hand to stroke it, immediately receiving a savage scratch.

Thirty years afterwards I was refreshing myself with a cup of tea in one of the same cottages and mentioned the incident. My hostess, Mrs Miller, going into her private parlour, brought back a photograph of the very animal. It was to her that the cat had belonged and the accident had happened in the very garden where I was now enjoying my tea.

A strange glamour had always surrounded my childhood recollections of this visit to the Durdle Door, and the sight of this imposing shadow of 'Fluff', so solidly presented in an enlarged photograph of the period, connected in a most reassuring way the very real present with the radiance of those past memories.

Animals come and go, long processions of human races – Saxons, Britons, Iberians – come and go. Merely to possess marrow bones is to possess material treacherously designed for perishing. Matter itself is not immune from these terrifying atomic transmutations. Yes, even the Durdle Door, that ancient hatchway of resistant limestone, honoured by generations of Dorset men and women, has little permanence. It forms but an image of relative durability destined in the passing of a few millenniums to be consumed by its contact with wild waves.

The White Nose

WHEN I first lived in one of the coastguard cottages on the top of the White Nose I was in considerable doubt as to my correct address. As a child I had been taught to refer to the cliff as the White Nore; on the other hand, the gate of the coastguard station through which I passed every day presented my eyes with the words White Nothe, while the people of Chaldon Herring were all of them confident that I was living at White Nose. It was this last judgement which eventually won emphatic confirmation from the late Mr Thomas Hardy, who said: 'Of course it is White Nose, it always has been called White Nose. You can see if you look that the cliff is shaped like a nose. It is like the Duke of Wellington's nose.' From that afternoon I have been careful to use the local name.

Although White Nose approaches an altitude of six hundred feet, it is not as high as Golden Cap, but both its position and its 'countenance' render it the noblest of all the Dorset headlands. This proud sea headland, conspicuous from the Esplanade at Weymouth, is a promontory of many mysteries. It would take a boy longer than a summer's holiday to explore all the secret Robin-Hood-retreats of the undercliff, the giddy ledges and castle rocks to be found in that strip of broken ground which extends as far as the blue slopes of shale where the 'Holworth volcano' once burned. In the winter this undercliff is entirely deserted, a forest abandoned to the partridge, to the raven, and to the red fox. In the early summer, when there are forget-me-nots in the turf by the cliff's edge, minute as the bright chips of enamel in a brooch, a pair of shiftless magpies translated into dutiful fowls of troth, give themselves to the exacting task of rearing young in a clumsy 'nitch' of prick-thorns. This happens during that fugitive period when the voice of the cuckoo is audible far out over the waves of Weymouth Bay, and larks are singing all day long high up above open strategic foot-square platforms where zigzag-figured adders lie curled for hour after hour in a voluptuous torpor warming their close dry scales.

Often I have walked through these strange landslide glades in the moonlight, and never have I looked upon patches of grass that have suggested more certainly old Celtic imaginings, so that I could almost fancy I heard 'the bridle's ring' of the fairy court riding by through the fresh seaside air which the scent of wild privet renders so softly sweet on an evening in early June.

There are groves grown thick with ancient elders, whose skeleton branches are white as marrow bones, groves where the old ballad witch might well hold her step-children under a glamour, the boy as a 'laily worm' and Lady Masery as 'a mackerel of the sea':

> *An' every Saturday at noon*
> *The mackerel comes to me,*
> *An' she takes my laily head*
> *An' lays it on her knee,*
> *She kaims it wi' a siller kaim,*
> *An' washes 't in the sea.*

Not only is medieval lore fostered by this majestic headland, its slanting levels are decorated with centaury, that beautiful pink flower shaped like a star, called centaury because its medicinal properties were first discovered by Chiron, the centaur, when he was schooling the heroes under the rowan-trees of the Thessalian glade. This small flower, with good justice, puts us in mind of ancient Greece and for the discerning the White Nose is perhaps more classical than medieval in spirit as it rises against the blue sky, so light, so marble, so well-proportioned.

At low tide it is possible after a scramble over rocks to round the dark base of the bastion until the curving bay to the eastward is visible. This chaste gull-haunted stretch of the Dorset coast can be reached by climbing down a hidden and very dangerous smuggler's path at Middle Bottom. This is an undertaking, however, only possible to one who still enjoys the sure foot of youth and a head unaffrighted by dizzy drops. Otherwise to reach the beach a man must swim.

From the shutter rock, just round the corner of the point, the deep water stretches only a few yards. Once across this the adventurer is rewarded. Here under the dense weight of White Nose is a very ancient and little-known cave. It requires no great imagination to believe that clear-seen Dorset is the lost island of Ogygia and this cave the hollow cave where the sea nymph Calypso held Ulysses as paramour for seven long years, perhaps the very cave where he so often received refreshment in the half moonlight; begetting his two sons, Nansithous and Nousinous, and where his heart yearned for high-born Penelope, his dear mortal love, and for the small rocky goat-grazing island, his native land. Out onto the beach he would go each morning, disturbing the patient cormorants, 'whose business is in the waters, to tread fisherman fashion the shelving shingle, his thoughts in far Ithaca.' All day long he would speak out his trouble to his own great heart, until at the fall of another evening, passing weary, he would return to the couch of the beautiful sea-maiden of the braided tresses, 'an unwilling lover by the side of a willing lady.'

If the White Nose hides strange secrets at its foot where the wild lavender blows, certainly it is not possible for a man to stand on its windswept forehead and remain dead in spirit. To the west across gentle meadows, across the sunset pools of Lodmoor, it is possible to make out St Catherine's Chapel raised like a goblin's thick thumb over the down, and further, the cliffs of Devon, and further still, on an exceptionally clear evening, Start Point. To the east lie, one behind the other, Swyre Head, Flowers Barrow, and St Aldhelm's Head – the eternal hills of Dorset.

The White Nose is so tall that it is no uncommon thing to stand in full sunshine and look down upon clouds lying, fold upon fold, as far as Portland Bill, as though a bed were preparing for a cloud-gathering god. In stormy weather, when the purple shadows are scudding across the Bay, it is the best place in the world from which to see a rainbow, a widespread arch with one ethereal end resting upon the crested waves, and the other upon the vexed grass of the downs, a triumphant heavenly arch with colours as dazzling as the feathers of birds in the Caribbean islands, as bright as scales of fish in Caribbean seas, and compelling even the most sorrow-laden to lift up their hearts in gratitude for the rich guerdon of the visible world.

A Bronze Age Valley

IF a wayfarer walking by the cliff path from Lulworth Cove to
the White Nose pauses when he has climbed to the top of Swyre
Head he will be in a position for scanning every feature of the
valley that lies between him and Bats Head, the next high promontory to the westward. The valley is a wide sunny acreage
snugly sheltered from the north by the ridge of the downs along
which runs the grassy gypsy track locally known as the Roman
Road. Chainey Bottom, for so the Bottom is called, taking its name
from an iron chain which was once hung over the cliffs by the
coastguards and still may be used by active people, is likely enough
to be, except for rabbits, utterly deserted. Halfway up its steep
slopes a dead elder tree is occasionally to be seen – a bare skeleton
whose paralysed back and crooked arms have been washed to their
marrow by many a south-western gale.

Herring gulls cross and recross the Bottom, flying in from the
sea, hungry for their ploughland food and then again returning to
fish, settle themselves upon the waves a little distance from the
foreshore, like a flock of halcyons buoyant and at peace. A raven
may also shadow for a moment the clumps of stinking-iris, the
sage, and the fine rough grasses that, during the hot summer,
become as yellow as the grass upon an African plain. It appears
that in the Bronze Age, and probably later, this undisturbed valley
was closely inhabited by man. When the sun is low in the sky,
either in the morning or in the evening, the ridges of the cultivated
plots of these seaside dwellers can distinctly be seen. There are

many such dividing 'baulks' discernible, and though the sizes of the plots they enclose vary, they are usually considerably larger than the amount of ground that today would be rented for an allotment in Dorchester or Weymouth.

Towards the lower end of the valley there is a well. Tradition connects this with the activities of the smugglers, and I have heard some of the older fishermen of Lulworth say that as boys they remember the remains of a false bottom protruding from the well's sides – a false bottom that had been constructed for confounding the excise men.

My brother, Mr A. R. Powys, was inclined to believe that this well, though undoubtedly useful to the smugglers, had originally been dug by men of the Bronze Age. He also suggested that the oddly symmetrical circles of flint that still are conspicuous in the valley, marked the sites of the village huts, built about with rough walls of flints sunk possibly a little below the surface level and roofed with boughs and grass. When the walls of these huts eventually collapsed the flints that tumbled into the saucer-like floor fell so closely congregated as to defy the encroachments of the surrounding grass, each advance that it made in the wet mild winter being cancelled by the action of the next summer's sun upon a practically soilless area, so that even after the passing of two thousand years the old position of the dwellings remains today as clearly defined as ever. The winding trackway used by these men for entering the valley is also to be traced working its way on to the settlement from the north-eastern corner. My attention was first directed to this remarkable seaside hamlet by Mr Salzman, the historian, who was for a short time a neighbour of mine at the old coastguard station on White Nose. He brought back one afternoon several fragments of Bronze Age pottery that the rabbits had scraped out. It is possible that there may have been some erosion of the cliffs during the last two millenniums, but it cannot have been very considerable and Durdle Door and Bats Head, those two sturdy deep-sea bulwarks of the valley, must have stood out much as they do today. The principal landmarks on the surrounding downs all have to do with the lives of these men of old time, either with their daily occupations, or with their deaths, or with their religion.

Dominating the immediate landscape is the circular earthwork marked on the ordnance maps as the 'Pound'. It is an enclosure, the broad round earth rampart of which would still be valuable for purposes of defence. When seen from a distance it suggests a miniature Maiden Castle, so prominently do its green sides, crowned with gorse and elder, rise up amid the acres of waving corn. Some years ago I examined it with Mr Prideaux, the late curator of Dorchester Museum. It was his opinion that the Pound might possibly have served as a primitive temple, and surely to lie in the centre of this august circle constitutes a religious experience. With the clouds silently moving across the firmament a man's nature would be gross indeed if it were not initiated into the very mood of these Dorset hills, so patient and so enduring in their strong simplicity. Here indeed is a place for the weighing of the power of the soul, alone, and, as it were, balanced beneath the heavens in one of those scales of ultimate judgement so dear to Egyptian mythology.

The conspicuous barrow called Woodwards Barrow, standing at the top of 'Tumbledown', a field of flints and plovers, is separated from the Pound by only a few hundred yards. This barrow was built by the same people. Let our minds revert to the afternoon when the mourners returned to Chainey Bottom leaving the corpse of their chief to pass its first night in a chalky grave. Several days must have been required to prepare this impressive tumulus for interment. The surface soil within a large circumference was probably loosened with deerhorn picks, and having been collected in heaps with the help of the shoulder blades of the same animal was conveyed by means of skins and wicker baskets to the centre where the great mound was being piled up. When finished it probably appeared twice as high as it is today, its present subsidence being due to the continual attrition of the mound through the usages of twenty-five centuries.

In the sight of God it is but a day since these men and women were living in Chainey Bottom, watching anxiously to see how their crops of barley were beginning to sprout, or to 'chimp' as we say in Dorset. On early spring mornings the Island of Portland across the azure blue of Weymouth Bay must have appeared much as we ourselves see it.

In every direction the higher ground above the valley is even now thick with the tools that these people flaked into carefully designed shapes – 'thunder stones', or elf shot, as they were called in the middle ages – in many cases never since picked up by human fingers! But the dwellers in Chainey Bottom were not only agriculturists, hunters, and fishermen, they were stock men also, driving the cattle down to water in the Winfrith, Lulworth, and Ringstead valleys; and herding them at night into the Pound – a place easily guarded by a few resolute drovers, resembling as it does the native cattle bomas I used to see in Africa. As with us, the sun would come up over the Purbeck hills and go down over Wyke, or at midsummer further west still behind the heather-covered Blackdown hills, where game would be almost as plentiful as in the great forest of Selwood below High Stoy.

Essentially the lives of these old inhabitants of Chainey Bottom were not very different from our own. They were stirred by the same emotions, by the same hopes and fears. As we love our wives and our children so did they love their wives and their children, and as the more sanguine amongst us eagerly entertain the hope of a life after death so also did these men, skin-covered and squatting on their haunches. Often they must have looked up at the Milky Way above the waters of the Channel, and, even as we do, for brief intervals have forgotten their day-by-day ordinary life, vaguely apprehending with rude imaginations the deep poetic mystery of existence.

For a moment, perhaps, as the soft winds, blowing across from the Chesil Beach, touched their foreheads, the real would seem less real, and the well-known objects of their everyday use – odd-shaped fish hooks and earthenware milking pots that they were constantly handling – would lose suddenly their insistent actuality, and the happy life of the sheltered valley, with the evening voices of children mingling with the wild talk of the herring gulls, would take to itself, for a moment, a dream-like quality, unstable as the surface of a vast tidal river that bears all before it, on and on, to a limitless and eternal ocean.

Bats Head

TO anyone with good eyesight, the great promontory of Bats Head can be seen from Weymouth Esplanade. It projects into the sea a few miles to the west of Lulworth, and far below on each side of its perpendicular chalk face lie two deserted beaches, the one to the east falling away to the Durdle Door, and the other to the west extending as far as White Nose. It is a remarkable headland. On afternoons of the wildest weather a man may rest here in tranquillity, some peculiarity in the structure of the cliff causing the rushing gales to cast themselves straight up from its sheer walls, so that the crest of the headland remains in an absolute calm. Seated on this halcyon ledge it is possible to observe in peace the riot of the sea-coast below; to look down upon great black-backed gulls flying in wide circles along the margins of the breaking waves; or to watch at close quarters the cormorants pressing their bodies in mid-air against the wind, their black necks tilted upwards.

There is something outlandish and forbidding about cormorants. Milton must have recognised a turpitude in them or he would never have made Satan select this particular disguise for entering the tropical acres of the Garden of Eden. How obstinate an egoism have these gluttonous sea-crows! Wherever they are it is the same, whether settling upon the water like mallards, or in groups upon a rock stretching out their wings like black fans to dry, or when, with the deliberation characteristic of them, they sweep forward through a marine twilight to their selected roosting places. What secret mandate are they obeying on such occasions? At whose word do these impious birds direct their unerring flight over the face of the waters? Bewick says that in some parts of the world men make leather jackets out of cormorant skins. How admirable to be defended against wind and sleet by a jerkin of cormorant pelts! In the reign of Charles I the position of Master of the Cormorants was a much-prized office – and no wonder. Who could aspire to a more impressive and singular title? Imagine the curtains of the royal audience-room thrown open and the doorkeeper announcing the entrance of so carefree a functionary!

In sophisticated subtlety the cormorant is not to be compared with the guillemots. There is a narrow ledge halfway up Bats Head where the guillemots have congregated in the nesting season for time out of mind. Here they will stand for hours upon their black webbed feet, nodding like punctilious mandarins at each other, until embarrassed by their own self-conscious manners they dive off from their chalky platform, and with their odd mechanical flight circle down to the sea. With us the return of the guillemots each spring is a recording place in the advance of the seasons. 'The foolish guillemots have come,' we say, as others speak of the first arrival of the swallows. What a commentary it is upon the brutal insensitiveness of man that these refined birds should have won for themselves the epithet of foolish; foolish, forsooth, because 'in their piety' they will remain upon their eggs until fishermen can catch them and wring their necks.

It is, of course, the herring gulls which through spring, summer, autumn, and winter, make up the real bird-population of these cliffs. It is their hungry call that first breaks the religious stillness of the winter dawn, vexing the waking dreams of the countrymen with their wild insistent crying, before even the red glow is to be seen through the lowest branches of the naked hedge. It is these birds which may also be seen walking on the grasslands in November, white as a flock of fairy-tale geese, or rising up suddenly out of rain-soaked stubble, like a shower of snow in a child's glass ball. At this time of the year they come in from the restless sea, from the ridged weed-drifting margins of the shingle, to glut their insatiable appetites upon the lowly victuals of the soil. Up into the cloudy winter sky they mount with their free strong flight, a flight so different from that of a chapel of starlings suddenly flushed and close-clustering as a swarm of bees.

How the knavish cliff-jackdaws are forever striving to imitate the balance, the aerial poise, of these incomparable white birds, and yet for all their javeline dartings they can never escape the ordained limitations of their being.

The White Nose ravens seem entirely to disregard all other fowl. Their dark shadows cross and recross the sloping shoulders of the downs, but they are always flying alone, the male and the female, with solitary, mutual love. In February, when they prepare for their first clutch of eggs, they are self-sufficient, and in mid-winter, when they come in over Swyre Head after a morning's scavenging on the Chesil Beach, it is the same. What a massive self-absorption is suggested by the croak of a raven, as it disturbs the stillness of a Sunday afternoon far up above the gorse and carline thistles. No wonder to primitive minds this harsh utterance seemed to conceal hidden meanings, dark occult messages, decrees of a dolorous Fate.

There is only one pair of ravens nesting now at White Nose. Each autumn they drive their offspring westward. These unnatural battles usually take place above the undercliff, towards Ringstead. I was once told by the late Mr Hardy that when he was a boy it was a common thing to see village people bless themselves as these birds flew above the thatched roofs of their cottages far inland, so that seventy or eighty years ago ravens must have been less rare in Dorset than now.

Aloof though the White Nose ravens are there is one bird that breaks in upon their proud isolation. For some obscure reason the heavy, dark flight of these giants of the air is exasperating to peregrine falcons. The war between the ravens and these hawks is as perennial as the traditional contest between pigmies and cranes. A peregrine falcon will pester a raven in its flight for several miles together, soaring high up above it and then with a deadly swoop darting downwards. I have seen them knock feathers out of the raven's body, but never do serious harm, and it is astonishing how the great bird knows when to turn upon its back in mid-air at the very instant when in its downward rush the peregrine is ready to strike. If the peregrine's attacks become too insistent the raven will fly to the ground, and whenever it is driven to this extremity the hawk will molest it no further, appreciating, I suppose, how formidable a weapon is its heavy, black, hollow beak – a true Saxon battle-axe!

Men have sought for the secret of life in temples and in cathedrals. They have worshipped in moonlit groves and before the sacrificial stones of monolithic circles. With closed lips and shut eyes they have waited and listened for God in cornfields and vine-yards. I think there are few places more fitted for such moods of religious receptivity than is this undisturbed sea-cliff. Here for thousands upon thousands of years the sunlight and the sea and the masterless winds have held tryst together, and nature, under the sway of so mighty a trinity, shows without reluctance her hidden moods, moods violent and material, moods of a severe and chaste beauty, and moods that are full of a deep and tremulous earth-poetry.

The Fossil Forest

IF a visitor to Lulworth crosses to the eastern side of the Cove, and climbing up the slope of the cliff follows one of the numerous tracks that wind through the gorse, he will soon be within a hundred yards of the Fossil Forest.

The famous platform lies halfway down the cliff and is easily acessible to all but the very young and the very old. It is a wild place of congregated rocks, blown bare by sea winds, washed bare by sea-frit, and parched bare by sea sunshine. Even in mid-winter on a cloudless day one can sit here as if it were the month of August, so absolutely is the gallery sheltered from the north by the shelving 'broken beds', and beyond by the huge mass of Bindon Hill. In summer the platform's heat is Mediterranean in its intensity, and as one looks from the sky-blue sea at the sea-blue sky it is easy to imagine oneself on one of those dizzy ledges that surround the Siren Island of Capri.

Nor is the Fossil Forest entirely devoid of vegetation. In crumbling crevices, and on patches of dry turf, there are two plants that grow prosperously – samphire and thrift. Both are plants of character, the first with its thick succulent stalks tartly smelling of the watery ocean; and the second, lovely as the old-fashioned garden pink, with a habit of growth so closely attached to the coast that it will wither and die rather than suffer transplantation for as short a distance as fifty yards inland.

Few people take the trouble to climb down to the Fossil Forest and it is likely that the wayfarer will be alone here with rocks, sea,

21

and sun for hour after hour. Even if such an adventurer should know nothing of geology his attention could not but be arrested by the petrified boles of the ancient trees. Lucretius, perhaps the most inspired of the old Latin poets, in a famous passage explains the appearance of the Earth's living creatures in the following manner: 'For neither can living animals have fallen from the sky ... It remains that rightly has the earth won the name of Mother since out of the earth all things are produced. For much heat and moisture abounded then in the fields, thereby, wherever a suitable spot or place was afforded, there grew up wombs clinging to the earth by their roots.' It was out of these natural wombs of fecundity, so he believed, that animals first sprang in their various forms. And truly, when one examines these extraordinary Cycadean stools they do suggest to the imagination immense matrices, so that, recalling the great poet's imagination, one can well conceive haughty unicorn and crooked-jawed boar leaping from such centres, new born into life! On account of the odd shapes that the encrusting carbonate of lime has given to them the fossilised concentric cavities that are uncovered by quarrymen on Portland are called 'crow's nests', less informed workmen of the old days having concluded that these fossil nests had at one time or another fallen out of the branches of the trees of stone which the excavations on the island so frequently expose.

The petrified matter enveloping the base of these trunks is some-times formed with circular ridges and depressions, which, so it has been conjectured, were originally caused by the ripples of the shallow water in which the coniferous timber was growing.

The massive boles that we look at in the Fossil Forest belong to the Jurassic Age. For this reason geological authorities calculate that since the period of the flourishing of these trees at least eight million years have gone by. In truth these fossils are of so hoar an antiquity that during the age in which they grew the ancestral fore-runner of men was no more formidable than a little marsupial, resembling the jumping rat, whose eager preoccupation it was to keep out of the way of the invincible reptiles who were then the lords of the earth. Even within the span of the Jurassic Age there went by periods of endless time with the salt ocean making vast encroachments upon the land and then again receding – encroaching and receding, receding and again encroaching. In lagoons filled sometimes with salt water, sometimes with brackish water, sometimes with fresh water, the dinosaurs took their pastime, dread, hairless dragons, abroad in the steaming rain showers, in the blaze of midday, and somnolent under the moon.

Around fern-like growths, palmettos and trees of the coniferae family, clouds of grey insects quivered and danced; but when the sun uprose from the ocean wastes, beyond where St Aldhelm's Head now stands, there were no birds with tremulous madrigals to hold the dawn under an enchantment. In their stead across the Lodmoor-like sunsets of those tropical evenings pterodactyls winged their way – flying lizards with the jaw bones of their horrid heads well fitted with jagged teeth and the span of their bat-like membrane wings measuring several feet from hooked finger to hooked finger. As yet there were no butterflies to flicker over the surfaces of the lukewarm pools or to settle with damask wings opening and shutting upon the crinkled bark of half-submerged logs. Everywhere through the wide levels of the shining sea the ichthyosaurus dived, more vicious and more voracious than is shag or cormorant today sharking for the flesh of fish on the lew side of the Blind Cow Rock.

Not long ago I was present when the shoulder blade of a plesiosaurus, found by Miss Woolsey and now in the County Museum at Dorchester, was dug out of the clay at Ringstead. It was an impressive relic of that time which outstretched man's power of comprehension. The newt with chilled belly and the dry sultry adder are but puny representatives of those cold-blooded, cold-eyed sauria whose dynasties remained for so long unchallenged. Those huge creatures upon whose plated flanks soft feather or glossy hair never grew, these pitiless gigantic lizards unprovided with udders with which to suckle their slippery young, in due time gave place, according to the inexorable ordinance of nature, to creatures whose blood by a novel dispensation preserved an even temperature however inclement the climate.

Aeons upon aeons followed, and then once more a strange instability troubled the earth's crust and the Forest Downs were lifted up and serrated mountain-ranges wrenched themselves across the continents, and presently man, separating himself from the other animals, raised out of the dust his tragic head of laughter and of woe.

It is possible today to rest at full length in a sarcophagus-stone at the Fossil Forest. Long ago this massive shell surrounded the wood of a fallen specimen of one of these primeval trees. Surely in such a coffin out of eternity the most frivolous mind should find release from time-imprisoning illusions, and exulting in the free gift of life, grow strong to contemplate all problems with a scrupulous intellectual integrity undismayed by the thought of death.

The Castle Park of East Lulworth

WHEN in the year 1929 Lulworth Castle was gutted by fire and left a square stone shell for holiday fools to gape at, Dorset sustained a most grievous loss. In the *Worthies of England* it is mentioned by Fuller as one of the two most consequential family seats of the county, and the Digbys of Sherborne Castle and the Welds of Lulworth Castle both receive from the cavalier parson of Broadwindsor, who, as the poet Coleridge observes, was always a stout 'King's Man', a little light banter. 'Lulworth Castle and Sherburn Lodge are most eminent, escaping pretty well in this late war, so that they have cause neither to brag nor complain.'

Lulworth Castle is still picturesque enough when viewed from a distance – from the sea or from the summit of Rings Hill – standing solid amid its wide well-mown garden lawns, and with its extensive undulating parklands lying behind it, for centuries the happy secluded pleasure grounds of its Catholic owners.

Today it is a dolorous experience to view at close quarters this broken monument of family pride, to see the masses of seventeenth-century lead still clinging to the dizzy walls, suggesting to a capricious fancy lodged accumulations of grey unmelting blizzard ice; and protruding from the same walls, floor above floor, the charred stumpy fragments of many a mighty oak beam that for over three centuries bore the weight of gallery and chamber. Once again the power of fire has been manifested and these ancient dormitories of privilege are now relegated to the chatter of saucy jackdaws and the screaming of the peacock tribe, preternatural and frightful.

Yet, though the great castle stands in ruins, the charm and beauty of the surrounding park is as unspoilt as ever. It is said that a man must walk a distance of five miles if he wish to follow round the enclosing walls of the vast garden estate, which include in their circumference ferny dales, hayfield valleys, and stately bird-haunted avenues.

Long decades ago, perhaps in the early eighteenth century, a girl was murdered on the road leading from East Lulworth to Burn Gate; her body was thrown into the deep pit still to be seen near the keeper's cottage in the south-east corner of the park. The girl's Christian name was Edith, and the pit is known in the locality as the Edy pit, just as the beautiful classical head bricked into the park wall to record the exact spot where the crime took place is known as the Edy head. A wayfarer who wishes to examine this sculptured stone must climb the bank to the left of the road, and, keeping close to the park wall, push his way through the brambles. He will soon discover the graven effigy not more than two feet above the ground. Though battered and weather worn it is still a beautiful object to look upon with its wide forehead so calm and clear. My brother, Mr A. R. Powys, suggested that it was a work dating from a late Roman period – a fragment found possibly on the site of some Roman British villa in the neighbourhood – and set in the wall to commemorate the tragedy, and with no claim to represent in likeness the features of the unlucky maiden.

The most attractive way of approaching East Lulworth is from the village of Winfrith. Half hidden behind the village blacksmith's shed is a lane running southward, which, with a few breaks, may be traced as far as Burn Gate. After leaving Winfrith this lane broadens out into a marvellously wide green way, medieval in appearance, and suggesting a track along which the Canterbury Pilgrims might have passed. Before the Enclosure Acts the people of Winfrith used to possess certain grazing rights called *Slights* on the Lulworth Hills, and without doubt their flocks made free use of the growing thoroughfare which for the most part remains now as a convenience for rabbits, careless of purpose, and for cynical foxes who travel on moonshine nights with an intention of putting the memories of the Winfrith hen-wives to a sharp test.

In the spring this rural road becomes thick-carpeted with daisies, as though February snow still lingered on this sheltered sward. At the top of the ascent, before the old highway becomes obstructed by overgrown blackthorn bushes, it makes a pleasant walk to turn to the left and go down to the cottages of Bellhuish. These pastoral cottages are situated in a valley whose peace is never troubled by harsher sounds than the lowing of cattle, the chittering of partridges, or the cackling of a flock of grass-nipping geese white as clouds. From Bellhuish there is a lane that leads to the north-west corner of Lulworth Park. Here there stands an ivy-mantled hollow tower of the kind that Thomas Bewick delights to insert in his tail-pieces, a structure built at a period when the romantic was artificially cultivated by the world of fashion, but which now, in the slow passage of a century and a half of winter nights and summer nights, has become what it once aspired to be, owls having consecrated it and generations of twilight bats having grown familiar, and again familiar, with each one of its crumbling bricks and matted ivy tods.

To walk under the beech trees at this end of the park is a privilege not easy to be forgotten. There is no tree that holds up a leaf of so tender a green as does the beech, and in October no other forest tree lets flutter to the ground discs of such fine thin gold. In the autumn a peculiar melancholy takes possession of these protected acres. The bracken then lies brown and broken, and dead elder trees lift white skeleton arms into the sea mists that all day long drive in from Arish Mell Gap, obscuring the grim gallows' rail where the keepers leave jay, stoat, and weasel to launder their bones in wind and rain.

In the springtime, the mood, the scene, is entirely changed. The japonica at the lodge gate is in blossom and the woodland drives that approach the Castle on its western side are yellow with wild daffodils, short of stalk but for their naturalness more to be treasured than their ostentatious cultivated cousins. No longer now do the flat ugly fungi on the dead elder trunks listen with their brown goblin ears to rumours of disaster. With All Fools' Day new hope has been born. Though the Castle has been overthrown the ancient estate still remains with its pastoral downland farms where life continues to proceed from dawn till sunset uninvaded by the present, and unchanged from the past.

St Aldhelm's Head

IF Golden Cap is the highest and White Nose the proudest of the
Dorset Headlands, St Aldhelm's Head may well be described as
the most romantic. I remember when I was a boy looking out of my
grandmother's house in Brunswick Terrace at the wonderful coastline to the east of Weymouth and being told by my father that the
furthest of all the cliffs, faint as a summer cloud on the horizon,
was St Alban's Head. The promontory in those days was always
called by this name, and is still so called by many people despite
the fact that a chapel dedicated to Saint Ealdhelm has for seven
hundred years stood on the forehead of the great cliff, a sure testimony to the verbal corruption that would substitute the name of the
martyr saint for that of the first Bishop of Sherborne.

It is known that Saint Ealdhelm possessed an estate near Wareham and that it was on this land that he built a church on the occasion of his waiting for a ship to carry him out of Poole Harbour to
Gaul on his way to Rome. This Saxon church in due time fell into
ruin, and yet by a miracle for all the rushing gales that drive over
the Island of Purbeck, a portion of its roof for centuries afforded a
canopy broad enough to protect the altar stone from wind and
weather and desecrations by wild birds. In William of Malmesbury's day, at the beginning of the twelfth century, the masonry of
this church was still to be seen and he recounts that even in its
decayed condition the building had provided shelter for generations
of Dorset shepherds, the men having learnt from experience that in
the worst storms no drop of rain ever fell on the sacred slab.

It has been generally assumed that the site of this church was near Wareham, but I would direct the reader's attention to the fact that there are not now, and never have been, shepherds on Wareham Heath. Folk of this kind are, however, as common as thistles on the downs near the sea. Here their figures are to be seen any hour like the forked letters of a black alphabet against the sky line, and, if, as I believe, the present chapel of St Aldhelm's Head stands upon the very spot where the miraculous ruin once was, the reference to desecration by wild birds would be particularly apposite, for the present 'mighty mass' is a favourite place for the sea gulls to settle upon. The evidence as to the situation of the original church exists at the British Museum in William of Malmesbury's own handwriting, and runs as follows: *Locus est in Dorsetensi pago ii milibus a mari disparatus, juxta Werham, ubi et Corf Castellum pelago prominet.*

The translation of this is: 'The place lies in the county of Dorset about two miles distant from the sea, not far from Wareham, where Corfe Castle also commands the main.'

Although the words 'two miles from the sea' go somewhat against our theory, the reference to Corfe strengthens it, for the famous Castle Hill most certainly may be said to command 'the pass' leading to the sea.

The story goes that Ealdhelm built the chapel so that he might have a suitable place in which to pray for good weather on his proposed voyage – and with such a preoccupation in his head what more favourable position could he have found than this high cliff-top, so much more appropriate to his purpose than any site in the

31

the vicinity of the low-lying estuary of Wareham? 'Sweet it is, when on the great sea the winds are buffeting the waters, to gaze from the land on another's great struggles; not because it is pleasure or joy that anyone should be distressed; but because it is sweet to perceive from what misfortune you yourself are free.' We have reason to believe that the Saint shared with the Psalmists and Prophets of the Old Testament the liveliest suspicion of the manners of the 'great deep'. In his essay in praise of Virginity he writes: 'Virginity is dry land, chastity a harbour, married life the open sea.'

The great Saxon ecclesiastic is fortunate indeed in the magnificence of the landmark that helps to perpetuate his name. What an impressive fragment of wild nature is presented by this Dorset cape! There is about the very approach to the headland a noble simplicity. As we pass from field to field we become more and more conscious that the tremendous stone foundations of the locality are only a little way below our shoe-leather. Yet this thin layer of surface soil upon which we tread is deep enough and fecund enough to grow acres upon acres of corn, the compact ears of which during the early days of August may be seen solid against the waves of the unharvested sea, gold upon blue! In this favoured month how wonderful to walk here! Every fleabane, every knapweed, every scabious and aromatic yarrow flower has in those prosperous days it own painted butterfly, and if you look back in your path in the late afternoon you will be able to observe numberless insects crossing and recrossing the warmed atmospheric spaces in a myriad dancing flights.

In the springtime it is different. The fields are bare then and few come this way. The Christmas shelters of the shepherds are still conspicuous in the lee of the long walls whose stones, every one of them, is hoar with crisp lichen. For these low walls with their bramble patches, elder trees, and signal thorns have protected the resolute bodies of hardy men through centuries of inclement weather. There is scarce a foot along any of these walls where shepherds have not couched with sacks over their shoulders and their thumbs greasy from the fells of the sheep they have been tending. They have waited patiently in these retreats, their honourable minds stubbornly obsessed with the case of this or that enduring ewe, which in a nearby solitary cote is labouring to bring a long-legged lamb, wrinkled and pathetic, into a world of sleet and the first Dorset daisies.

And what an occasion it is when the sea fowl begin to nest – cormorants, herring gulls, razor-bills, guillemots; and, above all, the puffins, sitting together like migratory parrots from the hanging forests of the Amazon, startling the sight with the tropical colouring of their broad chops!

It was just at this time of the year that I last visited St Aldhelm's Head. The gulls were calling over the sea, the larks were in the air, the wheatears upon the grassy tussocks, and I was alone. While examining the sturdy rectangular chapel a foolish impulse persuaded me to press my head between the stones of the narrow lancet window, the only window that the building possesses. A trap to catch woodcock! Try as I might, I could not withdraw my head. Very nearly did I become pudding meat for those same sea-parrots

I had so admired. When I did free myself it was at the cost of both my ears that were as sore as if they had been cropped in a pillory by a village beadle. A celebrated poem of St Ealdhelm treats of eight principal vices that pester mankind. The most exacting examination at the Day of Judgement will never find me guilty of Acedia, the sin of taking no interest in life. If this adventure with the window is to be attributed to a supernatural correction I must have been shamed because I have so often been guilty of Kenodoxia, a word the Saint applied to the condition of spiritual intractability that is productive of heresies.

St Ealdhelm was a kinsman of King Ina of Wessex, and there is something debonair and aristocratic about his attitude to literature. He was a great saint and a great gentleman, and, as the founder of Sherborne School, carried his scholarship with lightness and grace. This is well shown in his correspondence with Ealdfrith, the King of Northumbria, whom he taught to make Latin verses by composing a series of amusing riddles.

The ridge of the roof of the chapel on St Aldhelm's Head is provided with a circular turret for a beacon-light, as is also St Catherine's Chapel at Abbotsbury, both buildings having been used for centuries as primitive lighthouses. Is it my opinion that the existing chapel of St Aldhelm's Head inherited this lighthouse tradition directly from the Saint's own church, whose fragmentary miraculously preserved roof may have served all through the Saxon period for such a purpose. After reading the following riddle, the answer of which is Lighthouse, it is hard to believe that St Ealdhelm had not in his mind, as he composed the verses, the great headland that faced the sea, perhaps upon his own property, or, in any case, within easy riding distance of it:

> *High on the cliffs that front the thunderous seas,*
> *While the salt surf goes whistling down the breeze,*
> *Upreared was I, a solid and mighty mass,*
> *To show the sea-ways to the ships that pass.*
> *I never ploughed with sinuous share the main,*
> *And yet by signals from my lofty ledge*
> *I guide the wave-tossed wanderers to the shore;*
> *While murky clouds block out the stars of night,*
> *Flaming afar I stand a tower of light.*

Studland

AT the beginning of the century, before the townsmen of Bournemouth were encouraged to invade Dorset, the village of Studland was almost without a rival for its unspoilt, old-fashioned beauty. The approach to the sea was most lovely. It was by way of a lane, a typical West Country lane with high over-grown banks such as are commonly to be found in the Blackmore Vale. These damp high banks in the springtime would be covered with primroses, and in and out of the undergrowth warblers would flutter foraging amongst the fresh leaves and buds for a particular diet, their quick preoccupied movements suggesting the near approach of the nesting season.

This quiet unassuming lane never for a moment betrayed its proximity to the sea, and yet when one reached its end there were the dancing waves, the waves of one's childhood dreams, bright and blue and restless against the white sails and white cliffs. On the horizon opposite across the wide level of these sunny waters stood out the Isle of Wight, its proud marble gate that gave entrance and egress to a worldwide traffic clearly visible. To the right towered the Ballard Downs, bold in outline and terminating in a colossal fragment of chalk named by fishermen 'The Haystack', a fragment of chalk that the envious ocean had detached from the formidable mass of those eternal hills and which it intends, in due time, to demolish entirely. To the left on the further side of a low sandy cliff was an inland sea and sand dunes and a moor stretching far away to the lagoons of Branksea Island.

Memories of Studland remain with me always – the gorse against the grass and sea and sky fringing the coast's edge with banks and heaps of gold, the insistent crying of the gulls about the Old Harry Rock louder than I have ever heard gulls cry since audible from the road to Swanage and lasting all through the soft April nights – the glimpse I got of some Dorset deer on the heath, suddenly present upon the crest of a sandy hillock, their branched heads poised for one suspended moment before a swift and noiseless flight away, away, away!

I came upon these medieval animals a mile or so beyond the Agglestone Rock, a magnificent rock of ferruginous sandstone that has proved strong to resist the attrition of the determined centuries. Visitors to Dorset often question me about the odd-shaped stones they see hung up on the walls of our houses and I explain that no one of prudence in the county ever passes a stone with a hole through it with indifference, but is careful to preserve such fortunate fragments for the sake of the good luck they bring, fragments named by our Saxon ancestors Haligstan, and by us called Holy Stones. Well instructed have we been from our childhood by the 'superstitious, idle-headed eld' to venerate such toys of chance, whether they be so small that they can be hung upon a back-door nail red with rust, or like the Agglestone on Studland Common, of such enormous proportions that a whole cartload of devils, push and pull as they might, would be unable to budge it the breadth of a cherry-stone from its deep-rooted foundation.

Scotch firs flourish in the locality of Studland, and in August the air is often made light with the fresh health-giving odour that the warmth of an idle summer's afternoon can draw out of fallen pine needles. Three splendid hollies used also to grow not far from Littlesea Lake. In winter how their leaves would shine and how the hungry birds would gather about them! For years the second part of Matthew Arnold's poem *Tristram and Iseult* has been associated in my mind with those romantic seaside hollies:

> *In the smooth centre of the opening stood*
> *Three hollies side by side and made a screen,*
> *Warm with the winter-sun, of burnished green*
> *With scarlet berries gemm'd, the fell-fare's food.*

The longest walk of my life is connected with Studland. When we were boys I set out from Montacute with my brother Bertie to visit our brother Theodore who was then living in a cottage opposite the Post Office at Studland. Our bicycles broke down at Mappowder in the middle of Dorset, and arranging that they should be taken back to Yeovil by the carrier, we started on foot, 'on Shank's Mare', to use an expression of the period, for the Island of Purbeck. We passed through Milton Abbas and Bere Regis and Wareham and Corfe Castle.

Was it perhaps the Frome itself by whose banks we rested bathing our tired feet? I have never been able to find again those shady water-meadows, though I have more than once gone over our route trying to do so, and though my memory of them remains clear. It was nearing to the end of the long summer's day and we sat side by side refreshing ourselves by the waters of a crystal stream, a

stream as transparent as glass that flowed above a floor of separate
shining pebbles, a stream whose rich banks were thick grown with
comfrey, meadowsweet, and with purple loose-strife, a flower of
somewhat rank habit to which 'liberal shepherds give a grosser
name, but our cold maids do dead man's fingers call.' Except for
the murmur of a distant wood-pigeon there was nothing to disturb
the tranquillity of the sacred hour of evening, unless it were abrupt
intermittent splashing of a rising fish, the most cool, the most
happy of sounds! This vanished halting place of my boyhood's
memory was just such a By-Path Meadow as John Bunyan
describes in *The Pilgrim's Progress*. 'On either side of the river
was also a meadow curiously beautified with lilies; and it was
green all the year long ... also here, as you see, are delicate waters,
pleasant meadows, dainty flowers.'

It was not till the small hours of the next morning that we came
down the hill by the fir plantation to my brother's house. In those
leisurely days it was a pleasure to walk along country roads at
night. Motor-cars, inventions of Satan disastrous to every form of
civilised life, were seldom if ever to be met with on the easy
untarred turnpikes of the octogenarian Queen, and continually the
untrimmed dusty hedges gave out for a traveller's refreshment
warm puffs of the yellow honeysuckle's sweetest breath.

My father, though it was unlike him to do so, had expressed a
wish that while I was away I would attend a church service every
Sunday, and on this account the Norman church of Studland, squat
as a grey toad in a field of oblong emmet butts, became more
familiar to me, with its stolid walls and subsiding chancel arch,

than I could have anticipated or desired, but although by a scrupulous obedience I honoured my father's authority my own wayward inclination led me continually to the great Holy Stone on the open moorland. I remember visiting it after one of these Sunday evening services when a harvest moon, round and honey-coloured, was in the heavens. In those days I valued this ambiguous planet equally with the sun and would often find great liberation for my mind in meditating upon her wide sway. I knew that she was on that evening illuminating the free earth in every continent and climate, illuminating pyramids and temple gates, tusks of ivory and beaks of horn, the hair that covers the notched back-bones of animals and the hair that grows upon the scalps of men; even the criss-cross prickles of hedgehogs she was transforming into bodkins of purest silver by her bland and universal enchantment, the prickles of the sow hedge-pig occupied in edging herself towards the white dew-cold udder of a dairy cow which, with the simple dignity of her kind, would remain deep breathing and undisturbed while this lob of gipsy bacon was receiving its nourishment through the short calm hours of a summer's night in a far-off fairy valley by the banks of the River Frome.

Corfe Castle

WHEN I was living in New York City with my fortunes at a low ebb, it was my custom to breakfast every morning at a popular restaurant in Seventh Avenue. The noise of the heavy drays thundering by in the direction of the Battery, the distant rumble of the elevated railway, in fact the whole stir of the great city's life, so audible in the cheap eating house, would often be to me extremely depressing.

It happened that one day among the English mail that I had brought in with me to read I found a *Dorset Daily Echo*. I opened the paper, and the very first thing that caught my eye was a communication from someone living in Wyke Regis, saying that on a certain early date in April he had observed a cuckoo sitting on the top of Sandsfoot Castle and calling, or, as we say in Dorset, halloing at the top of his voice. This chance paragraph filled me with an overwhelming home-sickness. I could envisage the scene so clearly – a sunny April morning with the daffodils in every Weymouth garden swaying in the crisp seaside air, and with the cuckoo, its tail uptilted, fresh returned from the forests of the Congo, perched for a moment on the summit of one of the four walls of the old fort, its heart as merry as the sunshine.

Sandsfoot Castle was the castle of my very earliest recollections, and although in actual fact it represents a late example of this medieval form of defence, it has always seemed to me to possess a singular personality of its own, a personality as simple and as solid as that of the 'castle' on a chessboard, standing firm in its corner and amid other more sophisticated pieces.

Of course, I soon realised that Corfe Castle was of far greater historic interest; indeed, that it was 'the most romantic castle in the world', and truly I have never yet seen any other castle that has caused me to revise this judgement.

How magnificent this massed grey pile of heavy stones can look, with its tall keep still dominating the valleys to the north and to the south between the green downs of the Island of Purbeck!

What native of Dorchester, of Weymouth, of Wareham, or of Poole does not feel his imagination awakened when out of the window of a Southern Railway carriage he catches a glimpse for a moment of this familiar Dorset monument, its outline appearing like the dog-teeth in the skull of a dead wolf?

The late Mr Herbert Weld once told me that when the King of France first caught sight of Lulworth Castle he exclaimed '*C'est La Bastille*', and nobody could deny that the remains of the civilised pleasure house of this ancient Catholic family would even today, from a superficial point of view, justify the royal foreigner's quip, though except for its mural facade the Frenchman's exclamation might have been better applied to Corfe – with its grim insistent traditions of bloodshed and oppression!

In March, when the first white violets begin to show in the hedge-row banks of the Bloody Road, the mind easily reverts to the old story of the high-born girl out of Devonshire, whose eccentric habit it was to chastise her son with long wax candles so that he, Ethelred, even when King of England, could never abide these ecclesiastical symbols.

Attractive she must have been, for it was for love of her that the King's henchman betrayed his master and forfeited his life; and froward she must have been, with a frowardness that culminated at last in the 'foulest evil ever committed by the English since they came to Britain' – the cry of a murdered King and the tragic clattering of a horse's hoofs! 'And she wente to the Kynge and welcumed hym with fayne and blandishing wordes, and commanded to fetch bred and wyne to the Kynge – and wyles ye Kynge dranke ye boteler toke a knyfe and roof ye Kynge through ye body to ye herte.'

Today the race of jackdaws, with bright eyes and black, dusty, sunshine-smelling feathers, inhabit the dizzy ledges of the castle, where the same stones retain the same positions that they held when the voice of the worst of the Plantagenets sounded through the halls, the voice of John Lackland returned from hunting the tall deer, and calling for his meat.

It was here that Prince Arthur's sister, Eleanor, the Damsel of Botagne, was for a long time imprisoned. Scarcely in the whole range of our island's history can we find a more terrible indictment than the one written by a contemporary chronicler of the cunning and passionate King – 'Foul as it is, hell itself is defiled by the fouler presence of John.'

I have an odd recollection that has to do with Corfe. My brother Theodore many years ago was looking for East Chaldon, that is to say, for a quiet, peaceful, hidden-away Dorset village, where he could spend the days of his life in surroundings harmonious to the grave temper of his mind.

We were coming back from visiting Kimmeridge, and late in the evening of a lovely spring day entered Corfe to find the space before the inn crowded with people listening to an orator who was speaking from his carriage. We had not been aware that any election was in progress, and stood for a moment to enjoy the spectacle in the twilight.

It is as dangerous a thing to catch the eye of a politician as that of a drunkard, and almost immediately after our appearance we realised to our embarrassment that this prospective Liberal candidate for South Dorset had stepped from his brougham and was making his way directly towards us. A moment later he was shaking our hands with infatuated cordiality. My brother, a natural philosopher, is not easily put out by unexpected happenings, and it was not long before, with characteristic suavity, he had extricated us from our ambiguous position.

Another visit, scarcely less happy in retrospect, occurred a few years later when I examined the ruins with my brother's two boys. We learned the names of the Buttavant and Plunkenet Towers, and also we observed how the main streets of the village converge upon the ancient centre of importance – the castle gates! I remember we looked up at the two guardrobe shafts, still a conspicuous part of the masonry on the south side of the keep. These guardrobes, or ancient indoor retiring closets, acquired their name from the prevailing practice of hanging up the more valuable household furs in them, it being imagined that strong odours secured the garments against depredations from the moth that corrupts.

When I visited Durnstein a few years ago I was surprised to find that the castle where Richard Coeur de Lion was imprisoned resembled Corfe very closely. It stands on a hill of much the same size and height, and its forlorn ruins give to a traveller the same impression of the disasters of long ago. Perhaps during the months of his bitter incarceration, before Blondel, his minstrel, found him, the thoughts of the heroic, magnanimous King sometimes turned to his own similar fortification in the west of England, where his brother may very well have been at the same time plotting subtly against him. True it is that there is no river near Corfe, and even if nature had caused the Frome to flow through this break in the Purbeck Hills it could never have appeared as impressive as does the Danube sweeping by the little Austrian village on its way to the Black Sea.

Herring Gulls

IT is a happy thing that there still exist certain birds and animals whose fur, feathers, and flesh in no way can be made to contribute to man's creature wants. The herring gull may be included in this fortunate catalogue. Occasionally one of them is shot by some heartless gunman, but for the most part they remain unmolested. Boswell during his journey to the Hebrides complained of a bad night, attributing his insomnia to the fact that the pillow upon which his head rested was fitted with the feathers of sea-fowl. In England, however, our fat farmyards have usually been able to supply us with a sufficiency of bolster stuffing.

It is remarkable if you live near the sea in Dorset to listen to the herring gulls at the hour before dawn, shattering with their wild wilful living cries the august stillness of the downs. It is a sound that compels the imagination to escape from its contemporaneous limitations. These ancestral, pterodactyl voices, belonging, it might almost seem, to a maniac pack of flying hell-hounds, shock the mind into a remembrance of the planet's long travail, a travail that was taking place for inconceivable ages before our moment of time, and that will continue for inconceivable ages after we are dust. As the veil of the temple was awfully rent asunder on the evening of the crucifixion, so do these outlandish cries rend asunder the grey clouds of the morning's firmament. They resound against the huge bastions of the chalk cliffs, they twang abruptly through the twigs of each wind-combed thorn-hedge. If you are out on the hills at this early hour the first few sea-fowl to pass over your head will appear as black as ravens against the sky. It is only as it grows gradually lighter that their white ventral feathers can be discovered, though later, as they come to settle upon the green ground in the broad daylight, the white plumage of their heads and bodies arrests the attention as do patches of lingering snow in February.

In many ways the movements of these gulls are more interesting to watch in the winter than in the summer. In the months of December and January the downland valleys would offer prospects monotonous enough if the eye was not continually following the effortless aerial feats of these white birds coming in from the sea all day long to examine damp sods of turf for unlucky worms, and the bare platforms of the warrens for the remains of some rabbit done miserably to death by trapper or stoat, never again destined to scratch a lop ear in easy contentment as it enjoys the last hour of sunshine.

Down at Lulworth Cove there is a notable old fisherman named Levi Miller who seldom goes out in his boat without a pair of herring gulls settling on the gunwale 'to hollo for the guts' of the fish he catches. On one occasion these birds fought so desperately over the head of a pilchard that the old man feared they would kill each other, and, leaving his pots and his oars, went to separate them, pulling them apart by their webbed feet as a market woman might separate a couple of truculent barn-yard cocks. How bright these birds can appear on a sunny morning! What a heartless, natural beauty they possess as they sit screaming for their lucent victuals under Bindon Hill. The sunlight glitters and gleams upon each rippling wave, the headlands shine, the white sails of the boats shine, and the draughts of fishes drawn up out of the sea resemble bars of quicksilver.

Herring gulls are prodigious gluttons. It is a common thing to see them disgorge themselves after a surfeit. A fisherman told me once this odd story. He and his mate were returning over the hills at dusk after an unsuccessful raid upon a fox's earth when he bet his companion a shilling that he would bring down a solitary gull that was returning to the cliffs after a day spent in fluttering behind a plough's tail. The merciless shot was fired and the proud bird faltered and fell. Its body struck the ground with a heavy thud and before it died, in great distress it opened wide its coloured beak and vomited. There was liberated in this way from the dark dungeon of its stomach nearly a pint of worms, lowly prisoners who, as though they were little the worse for their singular experience, set about wriggling off into the grass.

How startling is the irrepressible vigour of life manifested on every plane! Dr Johnson once remarked to Boswell, 'No, Sir, to act from pure benevolence is not possible for finite beings. Human benevolence is mingled with vanity, interest, or some other motive.' If such a view can be taken of our tentative altruism, what room for disinterested action could possibly remain for these birds whose wilful yelps of self-assertion break so violently each day against the ceiling of the heaven?

If the chalk promontory of Bats Head be visited in the spring at the nesting season it is a moving sight to watch the desperate swooping flights that the birds make at the approach of a human being. A new note of trouble in their crying tells clearly of the selfless anxiety they experience for the welfare of their hatched nestlings, who, with quaint grey backs humped and fluffy, stand unsteadily on precipitous ledges blinking at their immemorial inheritance of earth, air, and water.

Stalbridge Rectory

I remember once at Montacute asking my father many questions about his boyhood at Stalbridge. From my earliest childhood every scrap of information about my grandfather or about my father's life at Stalbridge had been cherished by me. The mere mention of the name of the stately old Dorset market-town had the power of stirring my imagination. My grandfather, who was born in the eighteenth century, only six years after the death of Dr Johnson, held the living of Stalbridge from 1837 to 1867, and was buried in the churchyard there at the age of eighty, the same age reached by my father who died in 1923.

With the burial of my father in the Montacute churchyard it seemed that the family memories of Stalbridge must be forever at an end. This has proved far from the truth. Recently I happened to meet a native of Stalbridge, Mr Henry Habershon, whose passion for the village and all that is connected with it amounts to an obsession. I have never known anyone with such an infatuation for the place of his birth, anyone who husbands with such tenacity, with such depth of emotion, his long, long memories. The trees, the very stones of Stalbridge are sacred to him. As my grandfather was the Rector of his natal village for the first quarter of Mr Habershon's life the Powys family is closely associated with his youthful illusions. Here, therefore, against all chance I had discovered someone who preserved in his melancholy head an inexhaustible store of ancient remembrances, capable of being transmitted to me as clear as if they had happened yesterday. He described to me my

50

grandfather's carriage, recollecting even the precise livery of his
postilion, so that I was able to see as plain as in an old print the
coach starting away from the Rectory gate for my grandmother to
take the air through Marnhull, 'passing by little Charley's favourite
oak-tree', or for her to pay a call on Mrs Yeatman at Stock House.
From an absolute oblivion he could snatch back the very name of
my grandfather's dog, and tell me how when he barked the echo
could be heard by those walking in the street. He told of meeting
my father and my Uncle Littleton one winter on the Sherborne
Road 'beating the snow off the high hedges with their sticks', and
this casual reference, dropped without premeditation, seemed to
give me a glimpse of my father's boyhood as though I myself had
witnessed the incident with my own eyes, so convincing in its
naturalness, and yet so difficult to connect with the dignity of my
father's later years. He told of how my uncle challenged 'the worst
poacher in Stalbridge' to a boxing match behind the tall wall of the
Rectory garden, and how the men were astonished at the number of
rounds and the amount of punishment that my uncle, a mere youth,
had taken, and how when in the end he was 'knocked out', Mr
Habershon, who was bringing water from a nearby cattle trough,
heard him say: 'Don't let the old man know.' In a letter to me this
survivor from early Victorian times records the first occasion that
he ever saw my father and uncle, and for me, a man of fifty, this
recollection seems to penetrate into a past age beyond calculation:

'The first time I can remember seeing the two young gentlemen
was when I was a small lad going past the old Cross. I looked up
Gold Street and I saw a large donkey with panniers on its back and

one young gentleman in each and a man in charge, Sam Shepherd, who was living then in one of the Powys cottages on the top of Gold Street known as the Knap in those days.'

I came upon a reference to this very donkey – under what exact parcel of Stalbridge turf are its long bones even now turning to dust? – in one of my grandmother's note-books, describing how my uncle, when he was still unable to speak, would pull at his own baby ears so as to emphasise to my grandmother his satisfaction in the exaggerated length of those of the tall beast. She tells too with pride how my uncle before he was twelve months old would recognise my grandfather's step coming down the fine old staircase of Stalbridge Rectory, and would cry out 'Papa! Papa!'

Among some old family letters I came upon one from Dr Harper, the celebrated headmaster of Sherborne, the moral tone of which, so much in advance of his age, matches some of Dr Arnold's communications.

King's School, Sherborne. May 10th

My dear Sir,

I am always at home of sheer necessity, and it is part and parcel of my daily work to talk over such matters as those now concerning your boy. I am very sorry that he has chosen the army. I am always sorry for every boy who does so, not only because it is no profession in reality but also because of the temptations into which he is so thrust. However in many points your lad is fit for a soldier and will be a straightforward brave fellow under any circumstances ...

I am, dear Sir, Yours Sincerely,

H. D. HARPER.

It interests me to remember that while my grandfather was at Stalbridge, Lord Sidney Godolphin Osborne, whose character I so much admire, was the Rector of Durweston further down the Stour. There could scarcely have been two men more different. In spite of his academic honours, for he won a First in both the classical and the mathematical Tripos at Cambridge, my grandfather had an extremely simple nature, and I do not suppose ever had the slightest misgivings on the score of the social injustices of his period. Along with most of his contemporaries he seems to have taken the existing order of things as inevitable. He was, however, of a generous nature and gave a great deal of money away, never, so one old village woman told me, stepping out of the Rectory gate without a purse full of half-crowns to meet any unexpected call upon his charity.

While on a visit to London he met some of his Cambridge friends on their way to present a University address to the young Queen. He hired appropriate robes and went with them to the palace:

We went to Buckingham House about two o'clock and were in due time ushered into the Throne Room, where sat Victoria having at the left hand Prince Albert with divers other notables. I was fortunate enough to get a good place and saw the Queen and Prince well. The Prince is good looking, much like an English gentleman; as for her Majesty, I cannot say that her personal appearance is very engaging or imposing, but Pipsey will utter one of her indignant grunts if I speak with less admiration than she deems fitting. The Duchess of

Sunderland sat apart, retired, and looked a Queen, 'aye, every inch a Queen.'

The Ministers of State were present and on the whole it was very well to have for once been present at such a Spectacle. The Yeomen of the Guard and Beefeaters in the ancient costume were arranged in a picturesque manner in the Halls and on the staircases. The rush of the carriages was most awful, and the pressure through the gateways quite dangerous, reminding me forcibly of the contending crowds in my Proctorial Days at Cambridge.

I suppose I shall stay to Friday and shall hope to find my way back to the good old Rectory by dinner time.

I am your most attached and affectionate

L. C. Powys

On the occasion of my father taking his Honours degree, he wrote:

My dear Charley,

As the intoxication of success has now subsided a little, you can perhaps bear with the humble congratulations of the Old Folks. We are both very thankful to see you in so respectable a place in the Honours and we doubt not that this will be the beginning of a happy and prosperous career ... Littleton crosses to Ireland this evening from Plymouth. He takes with him the brown mare, by way of shewing her a little of the world ...

I hope your purse held out against the University fees. I shall soon expect a letter from Mr Perowne –

Ever your affectionate father, L. C. Powys

But there are more intimate scripts that used to be preserved in the tall study desk at which it was my father's custom to stand when he composed his sermons, and these writings show clearly that my grandfather possessed a deeply religious mind. All through his long life he never for one single moment doubted that he was under the care of an attentive deity. As a young man he had a bad fall from his horse at his home at Achurch in Northamptonshire and he puts on record his gratitude for his escape. Again as a man of forty, when he was a Fellow of Corpus, he had a serious misadventure. Sitting in his spacious rooms in the Old Court of the College – rooms which in my time were used by the present Bishop of Derby – he makes this entry:

Another providential interposition. Much bruised by the wheel of my gig crushing me against the wall but thro' Mercy not materially injured. While I live will I praise the Lord. May I have grace to use the life which Thou so frequently preserves to My Glory in Christ Jesus.

Lastly at Stalbridge in the cold winter of 1864 he mentions falling outside the house of a certain Mr Lewis, and inscribes these words at the end of the old service book that he used all through his life:

Jan. 20. Thrown down heavily on Pavement and stone step at Mr Lewis but providentially preserved from serious injury; all thanks and praise to Him who watches over His servant both in body and soul. He keepeth all our Bones so that Not one of them is broken.

To my mind, however, the most interesting of my grandfather's papers is a small parchment on which in the year after the Battle of Waterloo, at the age of twenty-six, he makes a formal dedication of himself to the service of God. 'So that I may become a blessing to my generation' is one of the simple phrases he uses. As a school-boy at Winchester he had spent 'idle and unprofitable days', and steadfastly resolves to live for God's glory rather than 'for my own selfish ease and gratification.'

This document, sealed with the Powys crest, seems to have represented in his mind a kind of testamentary declaration of the spiritual purpose which was moving him at that period in his career; and which, in truth, was to direct his life for more than fifty years still to come. To me the devout words on this faded paper, already one hundred and eighteen years old, seem infinitely affecting. It is as though I were permitted to look at, to handle even, the scroll that had served as my grandfather's passport across the Delectable Mountains to the very gates of the Celestial City!

In these days, when the hazard of life becomes every year more apparent, how restorative to take sanctuary in the sound pastures of such a village as was Stalbridge in Queen Victoria's reign, when, under the persuasive influence of age-long human usage, every cranny of life was well caulked with the honest clay of wont and habit and bright polished with the shining resin of an unquestioning Faith. Those long slow years knew no treachery. Clearly I can see them pass into eternity. I can see my aunt Philippa, my father's half-sister, the Pipsey of my grandfather's letter, at the age of eight holding in her nursery at Christmas time a reception for the 'poor old women of the village', like a silver-slippered princess enjoying the pleasing sensation of presenting each one of them with a new shilling out of her savings. I can hear the footsteps of my grandfather punctually every autumn evening going up the broad staircase, flat silver candlestick in hand. I can hear my father's very voice calling to his brother from those old rooms, and can see him in the pantaloon trousers of the day bringing in the first primrose for my grandmother, a service of grace which in after years he never failed to do for my mother. I can see him running along through the hayseed meadows of midsummer to inspect his eel lines laid by the bank of some dark pool of the Stour, careful not to disturb the corncrake on her nest. Where was there opportunity for treason in such a life – son following father, son following father, in long generations of easy circumstance, with the confidence of an endless sequence of happy reunions beyond the grave? What perfidy could there be in the agglomerate atomies that made up the yellow and black stripes of the September wasp's abdomen as it hovered with drowsy murmur over the last King William pear at the bottom of the silver fruit basket? It was my grandfather's habit in winter and summer to dine at three in the afternoon, a custom he had retained from his bachelor days at Cambridge.

There were no misgivings, no uneasiness of conscience about society as it had been ordered under Providence. Year after year my grandmother continued to fill her precious albums with spatterings of seaweed, with delicate paintings of spring flowers, of sea-shells; never, however, forgetting to see that Maria, the cook, put the tea-leaves that had been used in the beautiful drawing-room teapot out upon the wooden settle beyond 'Dash's kennel', so that poor people, by merely opening the back gate, could fetch them away.

In his old age at Weymouth when his mind was beginning to fail, my father one day mysteriously disappeared from his house. My sister remembered afterwards that he had said goodbye to her with unusual formality before setting out for his morning walk. Actually he had gone to the Weymouth station, and procuring a ticket to Templecombe, had walked from there to Stalbridge, presenting himself for tea in his old home where he was entertained with courtesy by his host. He settled himself in the parlour looking about him with a benevolent expression but spoke no word. In the late evening, thanks to the efforts of the station officials, news was telegraphed that an aged clergyman had been sitting for several hours on the Templecombe platform. He seemed to be in no trouble, his mind quiet and at peace, a happy old man who knew he was lost, but who was content to wait in benign confidence for the moment when he would again be looked after, again be found – perhaps by his daughter, perhaps by his wife, perhaps by his mother. I have often speculated as to the exact nature of the impulse that prompted my father to undertake so unexpected an adventure. Did he simply wish to revive in his mind old memories of his childhood, to remind himself for the last time through the sense of sight, before he entered the realm of dust and darkness, of the exact look of the mulberry-tree, of the chestnut-tree whose every bough he knew from climbing them as a boy? Did he wish to see again where his baby garden had been at the end of the nut walk, with its well-watered mignonette and large grave-faced pansies purple and yellow? Or as he approached near and nearer into his power, had Death, like an enchanter, cast a glamour over my father's faltering imagination so that he really came to believe that he had only to go back to the house where he was born to be welcomed once more by his brother, by his mother, and by his father, past all expectation clothed again in the sweet flesh of life, united and happy in those dreaming rooms of the ancient Rectory of Stalbridge in Dorset?

The River Yeo

T HOUGH the whole length of the River Yeo's course does not amount to many miles, its most extensive stretches belong to Somerset. Its chief source, however, is to be found a little above Sherborne Lake, near the Poyntington road, in the county of Dorset. The river has not been used too well in recent years by the townsfolk of Sherborne, but fortunately, through the blessed purifications of nature, it is still able to refresh the wide beautiful goose plains of Lenthay Common. From Lenthay the Yeo flows to Bradford Abbas, eventually reaching Yeovil through the Park of Newton House, and later meandering slowly on through the fat low country of Somerset, until, a mile above Langport, it joins with the River Parrett. Its actual source is known as 'the Seven Sisters'. A considerable distance intervenes between these springs and the ornamental eighteenth-century bridge which stands at the further end of Sherborne Lake. This bridge is an English type of those pleasure-garden bridges of the Chinese such as beguile our fancy on old-fashioned ware. I could, however, scarcely imagine a more English scene than is presented to a wayfarer who loiters here on a mid-summer afternoon – a scene more secure, more blandly tranquil, with the dappled fallow deer grazing lightly on the sunshine lawns of the park, with cuckoos calling from the trees in all directions, and with buttercup fields decked with brightest gold. I do not suppose the turf of these slopes has ever known a period when it has been unpressed by the delicate pointed hoofs of deer. Wild stags of some kind or another must have been snuffing at the air and gracefully tossing their antlered heads under the great trees of Selwood Forest even from Neolithic times.

How well I remember as a little boy being conducted by our tall schoolmaster, W. H. Blake, to look over the ruins of Sherborne Castle! This old Tory schoolmaster from Norfolk was, indeed, more of a country gentleman than a pedagogue, but for all that he had a gift for stirring our imaginations with a sense of past history. There was in his hall at Acreman House a stuffed pike, the largest I have ever seen, which he had caught in Sherborne Lake with a spinning spoon of his own devising. We little boys, in our white collars and Eton jackets, used to contemplate its ichthyoid countenance with wide-eyed wonder, the ferocious physiognomy, with sulky under-jaw, of this huge legless creature large enough to eat any of us up; which must have been the dreaded dictator of some dark water-lily abyss, sharking after, and devouring wholesale, I know not how many small fry, year after year, between Lady Day and Michaelmas!

The lake would often freeze in the Easter term and the school and town would come in Shrove Tuesday troops to disport themselves. The ice would be as smooth as horn and very black, and while the bigger boys, wearing their velvet football caps, joined in well-organised games of hockey, the rest of us would cruise about the pond's edge trying to keep warm. Meanwhile, far up above our heads, and the heads of the light-heeled crowd, carrion crows, intimidated into silence by the cold, would fly across the sky in the direction of Alexander Pope's 'forest' on Jerusalem Hill.

In the summertime, when the chestnut trees are all in flower, Sherborne used to seem a city most soothing to the senses – always the eyes fell upon tender, living leaves spreading themselves out against grey stones articulate with memories of a forgotten age. If Weymouth is the most beautiful of all Dorset towns in August when a thousand children dance upon its sands; and Dorchester most to be praised at Christmas when the town pavements are crowded with people come in from the country; and Bridport most to be admired in April when its solid burgomasters accidentally raising their eyes, as they advance down this broad flax-retting main street, become suddenly aware that the distant hills rising to view at the west end of the town have changed over night to a fresh parrot-back green; then Sherborne in the early summer is without doubt 'the flour of Cities all' in Dorset. Of it Leland writes: 'The towne of Sherborne standith partely on the brow of an hill partely in a botom. I esteme it to lak litle of a two miles in cumpace. For a dry town or other, saving Pole that is a little thing, I take it to be the best towne at this present tyme in Dorsetshire.'

Sherborne takes its names from the Yeo, being derived from the words 'scir burne', meaning clear stream. Yet how turgid the river can become during the winter months after heavy rains, as cold and chill it whirls past the leafless willow trees, sweeping violently round each mud-shelving grass-overlapping bend! What a sense of desolation it can then evoke, with small birds in dull-coloured feathers moving disconsolately amongst grey broken water-washed reeds, by the side of a grey drowning torrent, under grey clouds.

THE RIVER YEO

The sedge is wither'd from the lake
And no birds sing.

Again, what a transmutation in the summer! I have always remembered, as in a vision, a particular afternoon when I walked behind my older brother, Bertie, and one of his school friends named Blackborne. My Sunday top-hat was in my hand and I kept munching at the leaves of the tall red sorrel as the three of us sauntered through the paradise pastures beyond the Lenthay Wood. My brother and Blackborne were the two cleverest boys in 'Charlie Hodson's form', and during this walk our companion, a boy of remarkable charm, was gaily deprecating his chance of winning the form prize at the end of the term. Perhaps that particular Sunday afternoon stayed in my memory because during the next holidays my brother's unlucky friend was drowned while punting on the Thames.

Thirty years afterwards I happened to meet in New York a lace merchant, a gallant old gentleman with a curled pate and a courtesy of manner suggesting the period of the Regency. Recognising at once that he was an Englishman I entered into conversation with him. He was Blackborne's father. I remained reticent – for how could I hope to convey to the imagination of this quaint old trafficker the clearness with which I recalled walking by the side of the very boy for whom, as he confided to me, he had never ceased to mourn, walking by his side in what seemed to me a mirage world, quivering with yellow sunshine and hayfield grasses by the idle waters of the Yeo?

Cerne Abbas

IT is strong testimony to the Englishman's good sense that the Cerne Giant on Trendle Hill has been allowed to remain unmutilated throughout the centuries. We can hardly doubt that it has been in serious jeopardy during several periods of our island history, but neither piety, purity, nor prudery has proved strong enough to overcome our English reverence for tradition, for everything that belongs to the past. The terrifying appearance of the Cerne Giant is emphasised by the smallness of his round onion-shaped head and by the hideous spider-like proportions of the crooked limbs, while to over-sensitive observers the figure's 'brutish sting' symbolises the final triumph of appetite over intelligence. The chaste reticence of the monks must often have been outraged by the monster's figure as they looked up to it from the monastery. Many an honest Puritan must have eyed it askance from under his broad black hat; and during the decades of Queen Victoria's reign it must have offered an uncivil affront to the refined susceptibilities of the ladies and gentlemen, who in comfortable carriages smelling of expensive upholstery hot in the sun, rolled along the dusty roads from Sherborne to Dorchester. It is fortunately now out of danger, having been scheduled as a National Monument. It is strange to consider how this crude affirmation of life, deep dug in the chalk, overshadowed Aethelmar's Abbey from the day of its foundation in 987 till the day of its fall in the sixteenth century, and indeed bids fair to outlast the dream of grace the cloistered retreat was built to establish.

If, however, stark carnality stands unrebuked upon the downs, below in the village of the beautiful valley it is possible for a man to recapture the very breath of Christianity in all the freshness of its innocence. It hovers above the blue water of St Augustine's hallowed spring, evasive as the light from a triple rainbow when thunder clouds are in the sky; it envelops the ruined gatehouse waiting through long nights and days patient in its decay; it emanates through the subtle air from the lovely image of Mother and Son in the canopied niche on the tower of the parish church.

The last time I visited Cerne I was with Mr Ernest Moule, a man of wide culture and of natural piety. It was under his instruction that I was initiated into this open secret of Dorset and was able for myself to feel the indefinable aura of religion still lingering about these shadowed fields, now visible, now invisible, like the pale flowers on summer blackberry brambles, indeterminate to dim corporeal sight and yet their presence so soothing in the gaudy days of early July. We passed a shepherd in one of the Cerne meads sitting under a hedge in the shade of a typical Dorset thorn-tree, a thorn-tree whose branches had all been bended to the north by continual wild winds from the West Bay. The sun was shining and the man on this 'delectable mountain', with his dog and bright pastoral crook, was whittling away at a stout hedgerow stick as a support for one of his hurdles. It was impossible not to be reminded of the heart's wish of that ineffectual prince, one of the gentlest and most pathetic of English kings, who so yearned to pass his days in this very manner!

O God! Methinks it were a happy life
To be no better than a homely swain;
To sit upon a hill, as I do now,
To carve out dials quaintly point by point ...
... So minutes, hours, days, months and years,
Pass'd over to the end they were created,
Would bring white hairs unto a quiet grave.
Ah, what a life were this! How sweet! How lovely!
Gives not the hawthorn bush a sweeter shade
To shepherds, looking on their silly sheep,
Than doth a rich embroider'd canopy
To kings that fear their subjects' treachery?

And it was, so we presently remembered, this unlucky monarch's own queen, Margaret of Anjou, who had actually enjoyed the hospitality of the religious house here before the battle of Tewkesbury which ruined her cause. She had landed at Weymouth with a small French force on April 14th, 1471, only to learn of the defeat of her party under Warwick at Barnet, and beneath the sparrow-twittering roof of Cerne Abbey she strengthened her spirit for her last desperate struggle; her young son, so soon to be pitifully murdered, still alive and breathing at her side! She arrived at the Abbey at that period of the year between the time when the monks were heartened by the sight of the first swallow over their stream and the time when the call of the cuckoo is first heard from Dorset elms already in tender leaf; at the time when the woodsmen of the Abbey were treading upon beds of garlic in the forest of Nether Cerne, and ladysmocks and kingcups were opening to the cock-crow sun in the home pastures. What was the nature of the thoughts that floated through the head of this proud French dame in her Dorset bower of piety, as, with no sanctified intention, she prepared once again to fight blindly for the royal rights of her darling child whom she had suckled with the dragon's milk of her own white paps and was so soon to see stabbed to death by perjured Clarence?

With the sure inspiration of genius it is Thomas Hardy who has preserved for us in literature the very spirit of this haunted Cerne district. His romantic poem *The Lost Pyx* is charged with medieval Christianity. The Cross-in-Hand is the subject of the poem, that strange monolith that even yet stands in solemn isolation on the top of the downs a little to the right of the road that runs westward from High Stoy.

According to Mr Hardy this remarkable stone was planted here by an Abbot of Cerne to mark the spot where a miracle happened. This ecclesiastic in his younger days, as a hedge priest, had been wakened from sleep by a call to go to the deathbed of a labourer whose cottage was far away across the hills. The night happened to be one of those dark, wild, wet nights that frequently break over Dorset in the autumn, and the clerk pretended not to hear the voice of the messenger, but sluggard-like turned again on his goose-feathered pillow. Then in a dream the voice of God called to him, and leaping out of his bed at so magisterial and awful a summons he fled through the driving rain, only to discover upon his arriving at the cottage that his pyx, the metal box used for holding the wafer, was lost:

Then in dolorous dread he bent his head:
   'No earthly prize or pelf
Is the thing I've lost in tempest tossed
But the Body of Christ Himself.'

As best he could, he retraced his way through the pitchy darkness, sometimes on hands and knees. Suddenly he noticed a light shining from heaven and when he reached the place he saw that the hallowed casket was surrounded by wild animals from the Dorset woods. A stag from Honeycomb knelt by it; a grey badger from the ferny hollow of Glanville Wootton, the thick knees of its legs of uneven length religiously flexed; a sensitive witch hare from a nearby turnip field also worshipped; and by her side Master Reynard, the red fox from the bottom of Green Lane, with the red squirrel from the tree-tops; the stoat that knows no fear from his fierce face to the end of his tail tufted with black hairs, knelt shoulder to shoulder with his plump slave, the clover-fed rabbit; and the obstinate, flat-headed, self-absorbed mole was there also in 'pause profound', and a godless rat, and a shy, terrified field-mouse, with small, cold prying nose. From Melbury Bubb to High Stoy the rushing gale went shrieking by, but within the charmed circle of quaint prayer all was whist and still. These soulless unredeemed animals had gathered to adore and to preserve from harm this sacramental token of the heart-breaking mystery of life upon earth!

CERNE ABBAS

Then the priest bent likewise to the sod
And thanked the Lord of Love,
And blessed Mary, Mother of God,
And all the saints above.
And turning straight with his priceless freight
He reached the dying one,
Whose passing sprite had been stayed for the rite
Without which bliss hath none.

Stinsford Churchyard

I remember once when Mr Middleton Murry had driven over to White Nose from his house at Abbotsbury that our conversation turned to Mr Thomas Hardy's long life. My roving mind hazarded a speculation as to what had been the earliest earth-memory retained in the great man's head. To my satisfaction I discovered that this scrap of information I had reckoned lost had actually been communicated to my visitor. It was a memory very simple and so essentially belonging to the universal heritage of human kind that it might have served equally well for the first memory of Confucius as for the first memory of King Alfred the Great.

The long stream of impressions, so powerful and so poetical, that were to follow each other through Mr Hardy's mind for over eighty years, had their beginning, it seems, in the child's fascinated contemplation of the round shining belly of an enormous new kitchen kettle brought back from Dorchester market to the home at Upper Bockhampton by Mrs Hardy's mother. It was just such a first memory as Homer would have delighted to put on record had he had occasion to write of the hours of Ulysses' infancy, sitting with his nurse Eurycleia. What a long span of decades was to pass, momentous for the thought and literature of England, between the hour when the child gazed with wonder at the shining cauldron, and the hour when the old man's heart, that morsel of 'priceless dust', was buried in its silver casket under the Hardy yew-tree in Stinsford churchyard! And what a fitting parcel of ground it was for the burying of Hardy's heart – that heart which understood the mysterious affections of the hearts of girls better than anyone since William Shakespeare's time. Here it lies surrounded close by the firm long-lasting bones of his sturdy ancestry.

There are few walks in Dorset more pleasant than the one that crosses Grey's Bridge and follows the footpath through Stinsford water-meadows. How clear is the little watercress stream which, to use one of Mr Hardy's own phrases, 'crinkles' by at the bottom of Church Lane! That good man, Lord Sidney Godolphin Osborne, who at one time held the living of Durweston, near Blandford, tells us of churchyards so burdened and crowded with decayed men that they were abandoned by the very lobworms. This is not so at Stinsford. Here the dead are received with peace into the earth. To rest here on a sunshine spring morning among the celandines and long grasses is to be relieved of half the dread of execrable death. Surely there can be no great evil in a monarch whose wide scattered estate can include a plot so harmless, and so quiet.

How often must Thomas Hardy as a boy have walked along the riverside path shadowed by great trees leading from the bridge of Lower Bockhampton; running before his parents, perhaps, to see the fish dart into hiding beneath the green floating water-weeds, or marking from a gap in the hedge a crested patient heron keeping hungry watch over a shallow dike on the further side of the field. Nearly three miles must separate Stinsford Church from Thomas Hardy's birthplace at Upper Bockhampton. And what a dwelling this old house was! A large thatched cottage standing in its own grounds at the end of a blind lane, and beyond it the heather stretching away to Puddletown, to Moreton, to Studland!

I have been told that Mr Hardy used to read at the upstairs window removed furthest from the little wicket-gate that gave entrance to his father's property. There must remain even now many branches of the fine trees in the woodland opposite that have scarce altered their shape since those days, so poorly does the longest life of frail man compare with the leisurely longevity of mute timber.

One of Mr Hardy's relations, an old gentleman of over eighty, himself a poet of considerable local celebrity, has described to me how dear the heath was to his famous cousin in the days of his youth, and how there used to be a huge monolith standing in the bracken not far from the Hardy home, and how Thomas Hardy used to love the stone, often loitering by it, and how it was in the end broken up by some practical-minded rascal envious of such good material for road making.

This section of Egdon Heath, of King Lear's heath, has an extraordinary attraction quite apart from its intimate associations with the personality of the greatest poet of our age. The bracken here is so tall that lovers on their Sunday walks need never be disturbed by anything worse than mid-summer flies.

How delightful to leave the moor with its fir-tree spinnies, its clumps of goblin German-like forests, and go down to the rich meadows of the Frome. The water forget-me-nots growing at the river's edge are the largest I have ever seen. They resemble the blue eyes of children who, unlearned in betrayals, look innocently up at you and who never will forget! The juxtaposition of the lean, scraggy moorlands with those fat fields below could not have failed to impress Mr Hardy's boyhood imagination. On many an early summer morning he must have seen the milkmaids cross the meadows rendered mysterious by the gossamer mists of a West Country night, have marked them like so many Tess d'Urbervilles, pails and milking-stools in hand, leaving behind them at every step a track of scattered dew.

I remember one hot summer afternoon bathing in the lovely river, so glass-clear, so utterly different in smell and appearance from the sluggish waters of the Yeo, the Parrett, the Stour. Coming away from my hidden pool I had to pass through a clover field which was being 'fed off' by hurdled sheep. The shepherd who had the flock under his care was an elderly man with a typical Dorset countenance and a splendid ashen crook. Once when I was at Max Gate I had admired very much a small oil-painting of just such a weather-beaten shepherd. Mrs Hardy told me that Mr Hardy was so fond of it that he had always had it hanging near his bed. May not perhaps the small dim picture have been among the last objects that Mr Hardy's eyes rested upon, bringing to his mind this most primitive of all human occupations, associated for most of us with Biblical symbolism? So that the poet's final earth-memory may well have had to do with old scenes of penned ewes in fields of winter roots in the lowlands around Bockhampton, or with the fairy music of sheep bells on the far away skyline uplands of his beloved downs.

Round about me bulged the barrows
As before, in antique silence – immemorial funeral piles –
Where the sleek flocks trampled daily the remains of flint-tipt arrows
'Mid the thyme and chamomiles.

The Grave of William Barnes

THOUGH I recognise it as a form of primitive ancestor-worship, I always desire to visit the graves of great men who have brought enlightenment to the human mind. I would have liked very much, for instance, to have seen the huge stone at Delphi, so often referred to by Greek writers, upon which were to be read the awe-inspiring words 'Here lies the body of Dionysus'.

In my own country I have been fortunate enough to visit the graves of three remarkable poets whose years edged the span of my own days: the grave of Matthew Arnold in the village of Laleham, not a stone's throw from his beloved Thames; the grave of Edward Fitzgerald, the last of the Epicureans, who keeps his 'morningless and unawakening sleep' in the heavy clay of Suffolk; and the grave of William Barnes, who might almost be described as the 'last of the believers', and who is buried in the little yard that surrounds the church of Winterborne Came.

For many years I was foolish enough to mistake Whitcombe Church for Came Church. I even on one occasion explored its green enclosure in search of the poet's grave, never imagining that there could be a church even nearer to the roadside Rectory.

It was three years ago in the month of June that I left the Dorchester train at the little platform of Monkton and began my belated pilgrimage to the true burying-place. The summer's day was redolent of the old man's genius. The fat meadowlands on my right, golden with a myriad buttercup globes, seemed to render completely plausible the simplicities of his faith. The 'shrouded' elm trees and low-boughed oak trees appeared like ancient bards blessing the opulent pastures, with calm assurance prophesying peace to unending generations. My very bones responded in loyalty to the unassuming poetry of this good Church of England clergyman, who, though holding stoutly by the ancient pieties, never failed to oppose with all his might the oppressions of men 'hardy and industrious to support Tyrannic power.'

No poet in all English literature has done more to reveal the quality of homely village days as they follow, one after the other, against their background of the fugitive, recurring seasons. These bucolic poems, so innocent and so sturdy, instruct us how to become accessible to the wonder latent in every mode of natural existence, teach us to be grateful for the privilege of life on its simplest terms, and with firm purpose and serene minds, to face our inevitable lot of sorrow and death.

I found the graveyard of Came far more secluded than that of either Laleham or Boulge. From this acre of hallowed ground I could see English meadows lying swart in the blaze of noon exactly as they had done for centuries upon centuries. They had looked like this when 'King Gearge wer in Dorset, an' show'd his round feace.' They had looked like this when the maidens of Protestant Taunton had put on their white frocks to welcome the Duke of Monmouth. They had looked like this when Spanish galleons of Philip's Armada had been visible driving before the wind from Portland Bill to St Aldhelm's Head all one stormy dogday. 'He blew and they were scattered.' They cannot have appeared very different when John Lackland was hunting tall red stags over the bog-cotton moors of Purbeck Island, or even during the Junes of that dim century which saw King Lear at war with the turbulent elements on Egdon Heath.

Approaching the church past the home cottages of 'Herrenston' I noticed a date clearly indented upon the lead of an old, rose-mantled water-pump. I cannot remember for certain, but I think the recorded year was 1817. At any rate it marked a date long before William Barnes' incumbency. I could not but think how often his eyes must have rested upon these numbers known to him as well as the finger-polished latches of our doors are known to us, as, for twenty-five years, with his black satchel, he went to and fro for the performance of his offices in the small church. Often enough he must in wintertime have passed this pump when the ears of the boys sliding on the duck-pond were 'so red's a cock's cwom', the ruts on the high road full of cat's ice, and the 'huffing' wind caused swinging twig icicles to tinkle as he came down the avenue to the white gate. Often he must have passed it when the primroses were out in the copses and the gold of the celandines in the ditches beginning to show silver, and he would see little Dorchester girls looking for white violets on the sheltered bank opposite the turn-pike house of Max Gate. Often he must have passed it in summer-time when

> *A-vleen drough*
> *The leafy trees, the whoa'se gookoo*
> *Do zing to mowers that do zet*
> *Their zives on end, and stan' to whet*

and again in the autumn, in October and November, when the rooks 'wi' sheenen wings' gathered from the cold hungry plough-lands as early as half-past three for their noisy congregated flights to the King Rookery in tree-sheltered Warmwell. Many an aged body in his parish who remembered the French Revolution and the preaching of John Wesley this old-fashioned English priest must have fortified in the hour of death, absolving their sins with the wide allowances natural to one who had no love for 'hard words'.

Already William Barnes is but a legendary figure to the majority of Dorset people. Only folk of sixty years and over could possibly remember him walking through the streets of Dorchester in his eighteenth-century dress. Those who knew him well, the quick of his time, have long since been gathered to their fathers under the uneven grass of town and village churchyard.

The lettering on the Celtic cross that strangely enough was selected to mark the grave of this learned scholar of 'eald Saxon' is already filled up with moss.

I remember being told by my mother that when I was a baby she carried me from Rothesay House to Came Rectory that I might receive the old poet's blessing, and I find as the years pass that my mutinous thoughts are more reconciled to acknowledge the wisdom of a certain prose passage from the works of this simple 'inter-preter' of the fairest county in England: 'I had been working in my garden. The sun just below the horizon and the dew was already on the small green walks bordered by sweet-smelling roses and carnations. The stillness of the evening was broken only by the whistling of a blackbird. I sat down on a rude seat I had formed beneath an old tree and, as I thought of the fruits and plants that were ripening around me, I exclaimed to myself: "How happy if they knew it, are they that till the ground.'"

Weymouth Harbour

IF a man stands on top of the White Nose and turns to the south-west he will find himself looking straight down the entrance of Weymouth Harbour, the waters of which, shining like those of the Grand Canal in Venice, wind their way to the very heart of the old town.

It is remarkable how this river mouth manages to retain its romantic quality, encroached upon as it is by so much that belongs to the more banal and coarse aspects of modern life. Any loitering by its quayside can restore the spirit of a wayfarer discouraged, on a summer's afternoon, by the indiscriminate crowds on the sands, crowds that seem often so little connected with Dorset.

Weymouth Harbour, even more than the harbours of Poole, West Bay, and Lyme Regis, is characteristic of the county. It is the homely stable door of Dorset, solid and secure. A tramp-steamer may have been beating up all the afternoon from St Alban's Head against a west wind, as tossed about by the turbulent Channel waves as a walnut shell in a mill pond, but once she has rounded Weymouth breakwater all is snug and secure, with the lights from the taverns shining out on to muddy November streets where hungry, hardy men are hawking a few last fish in their baskets and boys are calling 'Echo! Echo! Echo!'

I recollect standing on the old Weymouth bridge one Christmas Eve and admiring the mellow glow that shone through the red blind of a Public House window. I have seldom seen any sight that looked more full of welcome. Here, the red light seemed to say, is a safe retreat where honest men can sit at ease on bare benches washed clean of all humbug – honest Dorset working men with their heads as packed with jests and old rogueries as eggs are full of meat and adept at trundling skittles and throwing darts as any this side of High Stoy.

As children we used to think of crossing the harbour by the ferry as an excitement equalled only by a donkey ride, or by bathing beyond the 'Red Post'. My father regarded it as a pleasure also. I have often heard him say to me when I had come to Weymouth with him for the yearly outing of the Montacute Church Choir, 'Llewelyn, I think we will now go across the ferry.'

What splendid types of British seafaring men have acted as Charons to generations of visitors, carefully ushering them in and out of their boats with conscientious courtesy for twopence! These old sailors in well-darned blue jerseys, with the undimmed eyes of gannets, grasp oars with their strong fists as deftly as a gardener will handle a potato spade – tough old men, they are of the kind that even death finds it difficult to trip by the heels; silent old men, full of proud reserves, who understand human nature no less well than they do weather signs over Portland – men who have sailed across half the oceans of the world and now rest old bones on the sunny seat under the Nothe, content to be able still to smoke shag and put bread into their mouths.

Some four or five years ago I had occasion to visit the Weymouth Customs House. It had been, they told me, in former times, the house of a wealthy merchant. From its beautiful bow window it was not only possible to overlook the shipping, but to view the

White Nose across the familiar Bay. The panelling that covered the walls was considerably older than the time of the South Sea Bubble, and suggested the safer days of a more opulent and more slowly moving commerce under the direction of substantial Weymouth burgomasters, burgomasters well fed on blue vinny, and with an unerring knowledge of a warrantable port wine. A friendly official conducted me into the attic of the house where was to be seen an antique machinery which had been used for hauling up the imported merchandise – sacks full of condiments from the Spice Islands, nutmegs from Zanzibar, sugar and coconuts from the West Indies. At Antwerp I was once shown over a similar house, a tall house standing dizzily on the edge of a dark navigable canal where men in lace collars had once sat fat by the fire, under the same roof with the produce husbanded from a hundred well planned voyages to the east.

The fine old corner house where Mr Board teaches type-writing possesses the same atmosphere out of the past, and the laughing young girls who each morning pass under the green lintel of its door, their heads full of gay contemporary interest, tread across a threshold heavy with lost memories.

The large, seventeenth-century warehouse that stands on the other side of the bridge, and which is now a furnishing store, is as firmly built as a castle, and its ashlar walls of Portland stones have been washed grey as the lichen on an apple bough by centuries of West Country sea-frit blowing in from the Chesil Beach over the dairy meadows of Wyke. There is a great room on the top floor of this ancient building spanned by enormous beams from Dorset forest trees, trees in whose branches squirrels were sleeping, chattering, and playing hide-and-seek when Anne Boleyn was suckling her baby Elizabeth behind the curtains of her royal bed. For age after age the mouth of the river Wey has been a centre about which human interest has concentrated. A dredge can scarcely meddle with its muddy floor but there are brought to light lost treasures of some remote period.

Today the fresh, brackish-smelling quayside of the harbour constantly shelters shipping that belongs to an older world than ours, poetical hollow ships of wood coming to anchor in this windless pool whose acreage is scarcely so great as one of the smallest water meadows on the banks of the Frome. And how many times in every year do sly old indoor spiders, and wainscot mice, in the houses in Brunswick Terrace, and in those along the Front, hear old men with newspapers held idly in their hands say, as they stand before the seaside windows, spectacles still on nose, 'The Jersey steamer is now coming in!'

But familiar to all Weymouth inhabitants as are the red funnels of these seaworthy island vessels, they do not have so close a hold upon our heart roots as does the Lulworth steamer, which, with its sturdy well-balanced paddles and its cheerful juggings and churnings, still continues each summer to carry holiday subjects of the King across the waters of a bay as white and blue in colour as are the arches of the heavens.

Portland

I remember when I was thinking of returning to settle in England on the Dorset coast taking down from a bookshelf in an old house in Connecticut an encyclopaedia containing a tattered map of Dorset with the Island of Portland stretching its bald bold turkey's head far out into the English Channel. In almost any map this peninsula must of necessity protrude as an emphatic appendage to the southern coastline of England, conspicuous to the human eye, to the Chinaman's eye, to the Negro's eye, to the Red Indian's eye, to the eye of a Church Missionary native idling over his lesson book under a palm-tree in the Cannibal Islands.

What a wealth of romance has surrounded this West Country promontory since the days of my earliest childhood! Its frowning forehead was familiar to me from Brunswick Terrace in Weymouth, towering above the magpie-speckled lighthouse on the 'old' Breakwater. Rumours of it had reached my ears when I was a very infant. My father used often to appear with round flat pebbles for my mother and grandmother to paint pictures upon, and these, I was told, came from Portland; and when the weather had been particularly wild I would hear of my father and my elder brothers making an excursion to Portland to see the waves!

I cannot conceive of any portion of the English coast more calculated to arouse a boy's imagination than the Chiswell end of the Chesil Beach. It is possible even when the weather is rough to stand in comparative safety and look down into the dragon throat of the terrible bay. A prodigious Atlantic roller, visible for a long time to a rain-drenched onlooker above the turbulence of all lesser waves far out at sea, dashes itself at last against this huge natural breakwater, and a second later, its pride broken, withdraws with an irresistible suction down, down, down, foam and tumbling pebbles together, until with a snarl the very ocean floor is, for the duration of a moment, exposed under the curved suspended arch of a tottering wall of water, high towering as a church steeple, broad and awe-inspiring as the Niagara in flood.

On a fair summer's morning how wonderful to stand on the famous sea-bank looking out over Dead Man's Bay, with wide-benched deep-water fishing boats on every side, and the pebbles under foot spotted and blackened with fisherman's tar; the air smelling of green waves, of wind and sunshine; and with vast nets spread out everywhere to dry, loaded with cork floats five times larger in size than those that dangle on the puny spider-web Weymouth nets, brown nets with a mesh so stout that they could drag to shore an entangled mermaid for all her petulance. And the old stone tavern called the *Cove Inn* which stands on the top of the beach – was there ever such a hostel? The landlord once told me that during the worst winter gales the sea invariably reaches to its stone porch and goes pouring down on each side of the house to the sheltered village street below. What a view presents itself from its sarcophagus-like doorway in fine weather – the great sea beach with its wide-sweeping curve of twenty miles, the broad flecked acres of the West Bay; and everywhere old weather-worn benches, old stone seats, where generations of aged fishermen, with bleared eyes still as keen of sight as the eyes of shags are content to sit for hours scanning a sea and horizon familiar to them for the past seventy or eighty years.

To a boy who has explored the rocks at Portland, other rocks will be forever dwarfed. Here are rocks large as cottages, and piled in such confusion that a child slipping through a narrow crevice may easily find himself in a secret chamber large enough for the storing of all the cheeses that a Polyphemus could husband during a period of ten years. In some of these natural caves there would be room enough for a Sea King and his debonair leman to hold high state, with fifty slippery attendants of singular but not ungraceful favour ranged around him on stools of rock, matted with seaweed.

It is best to come to the Bill when the summer visitors have dispersed to their distant homes. On a dim afternoon in November one can listen to sermons of excellent import at the foot of the pulpit rock. Thomas Hardy was aware of this or he could never have written *The Souls of the Slain*. On a winter's day the end of Portland Bill is a place of great solemnity. An eternal contest takes place here between old earth and her ancient antagonist. Year after year, century after century, millennium after millennium, it has continued, and its issue remains uncertain. All night long, with thunder and might, undaunted waves in infuriated troops hurl themselves against the indurate promontory which, whether it be daylight or pitchy darkness, remains sulky and unafraid. Meanwhile there pass by the Bill, clinging to the necks of their runaway stallions lashed to desperation by the whips of the wind, the Thuellai, women-spirits of the storm. They go shrieking over the Race. With demented outcries they scream at the four Trinity

House men on the Shambles' lightship, and pass on and on above the sheer chalk headlands of the Dorset coast, until the ecstasy of their stampede at last is foiled by firm-set sensible village windows and village chimneys, and by the bare boughs of the ash, the elm, and the oak.

Who has a soul strong enough to stand alone in such a gale at the end of Portland Bill, and witness the passions of this Bedlam let loose from the dungeons of unvanquishable Nature? Man is but a shadow, a scrap of unheeded flotsam drifting we know not whither over the surface of deep waters!

A Famous Wreck

IT is always interesting to trace a great man's association with the particular locality of our allegiance. We have in the letters of William and Dorothy Wordsworth delightful glimpses of the poet's stay in the old eighteenth-century house of Racedown which stands under Lewesdon Hill, in Dorset. The house was lent to the poet rent free by John Frederick Pinney, though Mr Pinney's father, a rich Bristol merchant, was left under the impression that Wordsworth was paying regularly for it. It was here that, quit of worldly worries, he was for the first time able to settle down to an existence of calm, uneventful days suitable to his temperament. He chopped logs for the firing, went to fetch provisions for the house, and once a week walked into Cruikhem (Crewkerne) for his letters.

The poet and his sister arrived at Racedown in the month of November, 1795. Ten years later another event occurred which was to connect in a particularly sad way the Wordsworth family with the county of Dorset. This was the tragic loss of the East India merchant vessel, the *Earl of Abergavenny*, one of the finest ships in the Company's service, on the Shambles, a reef of rocks lying a little to the east of Portland. Many lives were lost, amongst them being that of Captain John Wordsworth, the poet's younger brother, who was in command of the unlucky merchantman. The *Abergavenny*, during the morning of the disaster, had been beating about in the West Bay with her jibboom in, and the mizzen top-gallant mast lying on deck. At three in the afternoon a pilot was taken on board. As the vessel neared the Shambles, today guarded by a Trinity House lightship, the wind suddenly dropped. A strong westward drifting tide was running, and the *Abergavenny*, caught in 'the Race', was carried on to the dreaded rocks. 'Pilot, you have ruined me,' exclaimed Captain John Wordsworth, as he realised what was about to happen. She struck the rocks at five o'clock, while it was still daylight, though the February evening was already beginning to close in.

In the vain hope that he would be able to shoot the *Abergavenny* over the reef, Captain Wordsworth ordered the topsails to be hoisted. The wind, however, had now shifted to the north-east and was blowing fresh off the downs from Culliford's Tree. For two hours the ship could not be budged. With three or four feet of water in her hold she kept swinging backwards and forwards, now to starboard, now to port, as the force of the tide or the force of the surf took possession of her. So violent were the shocks sustained by the ship that the officers and men were scarcely able to stand on the deck. In order not to alarm the passengers on board, valuable time was allowed to pass before orders were given for eighteen signals of distress to be fired.

At seven o'clock the *Abergavenny* freed herself, but she was now taking water so fast that Captain Wordsworth judged the best chance of saving her was to hoist all sail in the hope of being able to run her on to Weymouth sands, though how he proposed to do this in the teeth of a brisk wind is not clear. The carpenter presently, however, appeared upon deck announcing that he could do no more and that the ship must inevitably go to the bottom in a few minutes. This news was reported by the chief mate to the

Captain. 'It cannot be helped. God's will be done,' answered John Wordsworth.

The *Abergavenny* foundered. Many of the men were washed overboard as she went down. Captain Wordsworth was observed for a few moments swimming in the sea, but was soon lost to sight. Where she sank the bay was shallow enough to leave her masts above the surface of the water. A shocking scene immediately ensued. All who had not been washed overboard began clambering into the hurricane-torn shrouds, after the manner of rats making the utmost shift to escape death. One seaman, finding his leg held by a passenger and the progress of his climb to safety impeded, took out his clasp knife and cut off the offending fingers, so that the unfortunate wretch fell back into the sea. A woman passenger, in her terror, lacerated with her teeth the arm of her husband as he was trying to help her to a better position. Shouts and cries and shrieks of panic rose to the heavens, a volume of incoherent sound carried over the wind-scourged sea.

The freezing gale continued to blow across from Bincombe Down, adding to the horror of the scene, while huge waves every few moments broke against the flapping canvas. An unknown vessel passed close. She was 'a sloop-rigged vessel with two boats astern.' She disappeared into the night without offering any assistance. Continually people fell from the rigging, overcome by the cold or the difficulties of their positions, to mingle with the bodies of those already drowned, which kept washing against the lower sails half submerged in the sea.

Small boats presently appeared and began navigating near the unhappy wreck, but out of a not very honourable caution they did not venture too close lest they should be swamped by so many unnerved men and women desperate for life. Slowly the wild, dark hours went by. A few people preserved themselves by balancing on floating wreckage. One man, the ship's joiner, floundering in the waves, managed to reach a launch which had floated away with the livestock that were to have been used on the voyage – sheep and cows. He climbed into the rudderless raft and was saved along with the animals.

It was not until the small hours that two sloops appeared. These vessels, anchoring nearby, succeeded in taking off the remaining survivors in good order, twenty at a time, and conveyed them, safe and sound, into Weymouth Harbour. Captain Wordsworth's body was washed up on Weymouth beach some weeks later. De Quincey asserts that he was buried in the Isle of Wight, but he evidently mistook the word Wight for Wyke, for the unlucky sea captain, aged thirty-two, lies in the churchyard of the original mother church of Weymouth, together with many of his own passengers and seamen.

The *Abergavenny* came to rest with twenty-seven feet of water over her upper deck. She heeled over a little to one side. The hope was for a long time entertained that she could be 'weighed'. Much of the valuable cargo was eventually recovered by a man named Tomkins, with the aid of a forcing air-pump, but she herself is still below the surface.

I have been told that deep-sea anglers who favour the Shamble 'grounds' often bring back to Weymouth with their catches of bright fish, encrusted souvenirs from the wreck. Generations of flickering whitebait have gone sharking through the gaping portholes on the lookout for their invisible victuals. Generations of conger eels have wound their way in and out of the jointed timbers. She is there summer after summer, when the beautiful curving bay is happy with visitors from distant Dorset villages, and when a poet can stand under the August sun entranced

And see the children sport upon the shore
And hear the mighty waters rolling ever more.

William Wordsworth had by this time married and had left Dorset to live, together with his sister Dorothy, at Dove Cottage on the edge of Grasmere. Richard Wordsworth, the poet's elder brother, broke the ill-news in the following letter:

Staple Inn,
Feb. 7th, 1805

My Dear Brother,
It is with the most painful concern that I inform you of the loss of the ship Abergavenny *off Weymouth last night ... I am told that a great number of Persons have perished, and that our Brother John is amongst that number ... The ship struck against a Rock, and went to the Bottom. You will impart this to Dorothy in the best manner you can, and remember me most affectly. to her, and your wife, believe me*
Yours most sincerely,
Rd. Wordsworth

This news completely overwhelmed the peaceful household for several weeks, and the letters written during the period are full of pathos:

We have done all that could be done to console each other by weeping together. I trust we shall with the blessing of God grow calmer every day. I cannot say anything at present more favourable than that we are all free from bodily illness, and do our best to support ourselves. I was useful to Dorothy and Mary during the first 12 hours which were dreadful, at present I weep with them and attempt little more.

Matthew Arnold, in after years, comparing Wordsworth to Goethe, charged the English poet with 'averting his ken from half of human fate', and true enough it was that Wordsworth had small experience of human misery and only knew of those natural sorrows which are sometimes named 'visitations of God'. The news of his brother's death shocked him out of his customary complacency and compelled him to reconsider ultimate questions. After so heartless a calamity, how was it possible to justify the ways of God to men? It could only be done through a belief in a future life!

'Why,' he writes, 'have we sympathies that make the best of us afraid of inflicting pain and sorrow, which yet we see dealt about so lavishly by the Supreme Governor? Why should our notions of right towards each other, and to all sentient beings within our influence, differ so widely from what appears to be His notion and rule, if everything were to end here? Would it not be blasphemy to say that, upon the supposition of the thinking principle being destroyed by death, however inferior we may be to the great Cause and Ruler of things, we have *more of love* in our nature than He has? The thought is monstrous; and yet how to get rid of it, except upon the supposition of another and a *better world* I do not see.'

In the same letter he gives us a glimpse of his brother's last moments as they had been described by one of the survivors:

A few minutes before the ship went down, my brother was seen talking with the first mate, with apparent cheerfulness; and he was standing on the hen-coop, which is the point from which he could overlook the whole ship, the moment she went down, dying as he had lived, in the place and point where his duty stationed him.

A little later in the same letter he quoted these words from Aristotle:

It is the property of fortitude not to be easily terrified by the dread of things pertaining to death.

Hardy's Monument

IT is often an interest to identify the distant landmarks to be seen from the high places of a neighbourhood. My own attempts to do this have been remarkably rewarded. From White Nose I have found it is possible to see St Catherine's Chapel at Abbotsbury, not the hill upon which the chapel stands, but the building itself, which, like a square thimble on a goblin's thumb, shows in all its solid perfection above the ridge of an intervening down. I also discovered that Weymouth is visible from the topmost crest of High Chaldon, a fact which I believe has been missed by other inhabitants of the Chaldon and Winfrith Valley.

Looking westward from The Pound above my present dwelling on Chaldon Warren, one of the prominent features of the landscape is Hardy's Tower on Black Down, the loftiest stones of which reach to the height of eight hundred and fifty-nine feet above the sea level. With field-glasses it is possible on a clear day to examine from The Pound the masonry of the celebrated monument as though it stood but a mile away. There are those who regard this lucky unicorn's horn of the county as unsightly, but I have never shared this judgement, so well does the structure seem to serve its purpose, standing sensible and firm on the top of Blagdon, as conspicuous to Farmer Shuttler's shepherd snuffing at the dawn from the door of his January lambing hut on the Breeches above West Lulworth, as to the hungry cabin boy swabbing down a deck in Portland Harbour, his ear cocked for the breakfast call.

Black Down may well be likened to the Somersetshire Quantocks, a Quantocks in miniature, with undisturbed moorland glens, gently sloping down to the valleys below. Thorn trees may be seen growing upon Black Down that may well have been good timber when George III was visiting at Weymouth, trees whose gnarled and weathered branches still are able to adorn themselves with odorous blossoms at each return of the spring, trees that have stood for decade after decade unnoticed and unadmired beneath an endless procession of soft grey clouds driving in from the West Bay. Trees of this kind serve as trysting places on these deserted hills. Ruth and her faithless lover in Wordsworth's poem must have often chosen such stark May bushes for the assignations of their wild romance. Just as the Quantock heather is of a finer and more luxurious variety than Exmoor heather, so the heather on Black Down surpasses in its habit of growth the heather which supplies Egdon Heath with its ragged winter jacket. It is the same with the bracken. The fronds of these ferns, with their vigorous antique smell, grow very tall here, and their rich green levels, warmed by a dog-day sun, and rising one above the other, afford the securest possible shelter for holiday lovers out of concert with the crowds of a motor-car world.

One of the most poetical of all the passages in Thomas Hardy's *The Dynasts* is that which portrays the death of Nelson. The last hour of the great Admiral has come, and he lies below deck in the *Victory*'s narrow cockpit, a dim cockpit smelling of candle grease, of gunpowder, of cordials, and of the wounds of disabled seamen. He calls for Captain Hardy, and the two friends talk together of the chances of the famous sea-fight, of Lady Hamilton and the little Horatia; and then there falls between them a long silence, broken at the last by the Admiral's voice, his face now 'pinched and wan with suffering.'

NELSON (suddenly): *What are you thinking, that you speak no word?*

HARDY (waking from a short reverie): *Thoughts all confused, my Lord; their needs on deck,*
Your own sad state, and your unrivalled past;
Mixed up with flashes of old things afar –
Old childish things at home, down Wessex way,
In the snug village under Blackdon Hill
Where I was born. The tumbling stream, the garden,
The placid look of the grey dial there,
Marking unconsciously this bloody hour,
And the red apples on my father's trees,
Just now full ripe.

As a matter of fact, the poet was not strictly accurate in assigning to Portesham the honour of being the birthplace of the flagship's captain. Thomas Masterman Hardy, or Admiral Hardy as he became later, was born at Kingston Russell in the year 1769 – the same birth year as that of Napoleon and the Duke of Wellington – and only came to Portesham as a boy of nine when his father, Joseph Hardy, removed his family to his small house there, along with the old dial mentioned in *The Dynasts*, still to be seen in the garden of the present representative of the family, Mr Hardy Manfield:

> *Joseph Hardy, Esq.,*
> *Kingston Russell, Lat. 50. 45*
> *1767*
> *Fugio fuge*

As an undergraduate at Cambridge I remember very well being corrected by Mr Charles Moule, the senior Fellow of Corpus, for mispronouncing the name of Hardy's village. 'Only bagmen,' he declared, 'call it Portesham. The name of the village should be pronounced Po'sham.' I never forgot what he said – for who could be better informed on such a matter than this eminent son of the great and good Fordington vicar, whose children included the late Bishop of Durham, the late Curator of the Dorchester Museum, the late Archdeacon of China, and Mr Charles Moule, a scholar of European reputation – all of them well known in the county.

Mr Moule's ruling finds support in the correspondence of Admiral Hardy, who, when with the fleet, was continually pre-occupied with getting fresh supplies of Dorset beer, 'the best ever drunk', to his ship, and who in his letters always alludes to his village as 'Possum'.

This 'Masterman Ready' was surely a true son of Dorset, born at Kingston Russell, educated at Milton Grammar School, 'The Eton of the West', and spending his boyhood holidays at Portesham. It is pleasant to think of those schoolboy years, before he went to sea as 'Captain's servant' on H.M. brig *Helena*, sailing under the command of his father's neighbour, Roberts, of Burton Bradstock – years spent roaming over the wild country about his home, climbing upon the oval slab of the Helstone, playing with his companions about 'The Grey Mare and her Colts', and netting Christmas rabbits in the quarries of Bronkham Hill – his eyes forever bewitched by the restless white horses in Deadman's Bay and under the long line of chalk cliffs, white waves eloquent of adventure and of sailor-boys returning to their Dorset homes after the hazards of the sea. Neither the old sundial in the garden, nor the stream chattering by, nor the dim image on the outside wall of the village church, was able to give the least hint as to the honourable fortune held in store for him, was able to divulge the secret that in due time a lofty tower seventy feet high would be erected 'on his own land' to overlook the Channel in fine weather and foul, and serve as a perpetual landmark for the fishermen and farm-labourers of his beloved Dorset.

The Swannery Bell at Abbotsbury

THERE are many odd objects in Dorset which, though of no intrinsic value in themselves, might yet conceivably be treasured by the older inhabitants of the county, simple objects which have through the passing of years gathered to themselves happy associations. Of such inconspicuous Dorset objects the bell that admits visitors into Lord Ilchester's Swannery at Abbotsbury might take a place. Which of us has not stood impatiently at the familiar postern awaiting the moment when we would step out of an ordinary English hayfield into a garden of smooth tropical lawns overshadowed by waving reeds, lawns offering glimpses of inlets and lagoons where shining surfaces might, so it seems, at any moment be disturbed by a hippopotamus protruding a bristled chin out of the brackish water.

When I lived in Africa my mud hut used to be overgrown the year round with geraniums, and all through the hours, in the hot sunshine, humming birds with feathers as bright and varied as flowers used to keep darting and quivering against the broad leaves and gay petals of the sun-loving plants. This was a sight calculated to rouse the dullest spirit to a vibrant awareness of earth-existence, a sight, however, not more worshipful than the one I was once shown in this Dorset reserve – a reed warbler's nest suspended by delicate cables between two rushes swaying in the wind.

It is difficult to share the popular enthusiasm over the celebrated decoy. Most surely the contrivance testifies to the ingenuity of the human mind, but there is little joy to be derived from contemplating the initial treachery, and still less the culminating confusion at the decoy's end with its subsequent massacre of so many free, night-flying migratory birds. I have always admired the short stories of Guy de Maupassant. This great Frenchman wrote of life without fear. As a young man I especially appreciated the more erotic of his tales, so full of salt and cynicism. Once, as I idly turned over a collection of his works my notice was arrested by a story that had for its title the single word 'Love'. I began reading it – and behold, the passion which this imaginative realist was treating was no human passion. The story described two sportsmen going out in the fens to shoot wild duck on an early winter's morning. The keen east wind, the distant booming of the contracting ice, the crisp ground, all were clearly evoked, but especially the devotion of a drake for his shot mate, as he fearlessly circled nearer and nearer to the guns over the place where she lay mortally wounded. This then is what I had happened upon instead of harlotry, and this story I regard as one of the most moving I have ever read. I was reminded of it when in Africa I saw a stallion zebra trotting around the dead body of his mare to keep the vultures away, which, in disconsolate rows, were sitting about the striped carcass.

I have been told that the two swans generally to be seen on the lawns at Abbotsbury have been together in content for many years, neither of them, so strong is the love they feel the one for the other, having known what it is to be restless though the sun shine never so bright on a spring morning. Mr Ernest Moule once told me that in China the fidelity of birds is so highly appreciated that it is the custom of the country to carry a goose before every bridal party, the ancient inhabitants of our farmyards being regarded in the Far East as a veritable symbol of matrimonial felicity. We in England are more accustomed to think of the goose as an emblem of folly. Chaucer, wishing to show how the tongue of a woman can extricate her from any situation, however awkward, makes her say:

> *Al had a man seen a thing with both his eyes*
> *Yet shall we wymmen visage it hardly,*
> *And wepe, and swere, and chide subtilly,*
> *So that ye man schall be as lewd as gees.*

The word 'lewd' is here used in its original meaning of ignorant, the passage suggesting that men, even in the face of the evidence of their own eyes, shall still, because of the brazen effrontery of women, remain ignorant as to what is taking place.

What a proud and sovereign bird is a swan! And how romantic the sound that comes from them in their passage across the Lodmoor sky in midwinter, their outstretched necks obedient to an infallible compass! When I was last in Weymouth I directed my bath-chair man to take me to the backwater that I might observe the swans at my leisure. Small wonder this bird has been a delight to poets from the earliest ages, and easy it is to understand how Leda allowed herself to be betrayed.

The Swannery at Abbotsbury is interesting to visit through all the summer months, though perhaps most so in the mating season. It is true, however, that swans on the land lose much of their majesty, the shortness of their legs giving them something of a waddling gait. This fact did not escape Chaucer's observant eye, and he hits off his roguish monk thus: 'Like Jovynian, Fat as a whal, and walken as a swan.'

It is a deplorable commentary upon the insensibility of our race that neither beauty of form nor grace of spirit has ever preserved any edible creature from our curious, shameless and insatiable appetites. The swan-herd on one of my visits pointed out to me a number of cygnets that were being nourished on a special diet 'for his Lordship's table'.

So it has ever been. Swans, larks – into our pots they must go, and God bless them!

> *Now certainly he was a fair prelate;*
> *He was not pale as a forpyned ghost,*
> *A fat swan loved he best of any roast.*

It does us more honour to remember the inspired works of laudation that our poets have given to this superb bird. Ben Jonson in his famous song to the Goddess of Love writes:

> *Have you seen but a bright lily grow*
> *Before rude hands have touch'd it?*
> *Have you mark'd but the fall of the snow*
> *Before the soil hath smutch'd it?*
> *Have you felt the wool of beaver*
> *Or swan's down ever?*

THE SWANNERY BELL AT ABBOTSBURY

And Edmund Spenser has made, of course, the spectacle of swans on the Thames immortal:

So purely white they were,
That even the gentle streame, the which they bare
Seem'd foule to them, and bad his billowes spare
To wet their silken feathers, least they might
Soyle their fayre plumes with water not so fayre.

When I was taken as a very small boy to wait outside the Swannery door I was reminded, I remember, of a picture in one of my nursery books, and this 'Beauty and the Beast' association always comes back to me when I have occasion to refer to the Swannery. Yet how different it actually was from my fancies, when, our ringing at last answered, we were admitted into the Beast's garden! In the distance were innumerable forms in dazzling white as though a host of angels with folded wings were gathered upon the grass banks of the River of Life!

Lyme Regis

THE coastline of the county of Dorset is guarded on its eastern and western extremities by two sturdy towns, Poole and Lyme Regis, which have always been as truculent as they are ancient. Few who have attempted to meddle with their liberties have done so with impunity. They are far-famed for their breed of honest seamen with a smack of the land about them – trawling fishermen, who can make themselves handy in a hayfield, and yet for all that they can use a pick well, can pull at an oar better. During the Civil War both Poole and Lyme Regis were brisk for the cause of Parliament, and an historian of those times reports that when Prince Maurice had reduced all the rest of Dorset these two small towns 'returned so peremptory a refusal to the Prince's summons that his Highness resolved not to attack them.'

Perhaps it is the Cobb, the extraordinary Breakwater of the royal city of Lyme Regis, that helps to give to the place its idiosyncratic character. If you look down upon this old structure from the hills above, it takes on the appearance of a vole's flat tail left dangling on the water outside its slippery retreat. The old monosyllabic word Cobb in medieval times had many uses. A male herring was called a Cobb, a black-backed gull, a miller's thumb; and with no great stretch of the imagination the Breakwater today may in truth be thought to resemble the king digit of the miller's 'cluster o' vive'. It is probable, however, that this odd barricade against the Channel waves earned its name from actually being 'a rounded heap of stones'. The Cobb was first built in the reign of Edward I, and it is likely enough that it would be possible to find at sea level in its marrowbone, so to speak, massy rocks whose fate has been as uneventful and unchanged as has that of the 'stolen stone' of Longshanks over which seven hundred dusty centuries have passed in Westminster Abbey as it were in a day.

With the Cobb on one side, the church on the other, and with its principal thoroughfare winding sideways down from the high hill behind, a very compact and solid seaside town is presented to the traveller who is exploring for the first time this furthermost corner of Dorset. There still exist in Lyme Regis small bow-windows against the panes of which, during the stormy months of autumn, quiet Victorian ladies may be seen standing to draw their thick winter curtains; while in the sweet months of spring and summer these same rounded bottle-glass partitions present to the passerby the angel faces of idle children, bright with seaside sunshine.

When Tennyson visited Lyme Regis people were eager to show him the place where Monmouth landed. 'Don't talk to me of the Duke of Monmouth,' he said impatiently. 'Show me the exact spot where Louisa Musgrove fell!' I have never thought much of this anecdote. The poet was putting too high a value upon the craft of imaginative fiction. The interest to be attached to the phantoms of literary invention can never be compared to that which belongs to men and women who have actually lived, even though, as in this case, the hero of the piece was but a sorry Prince, with cosmetics in his silken fob, the bastard child of 'bold brown Lucy Walters'.

On several occasions my father elected to visit Lyme Regis for his yearly holiday, travelling from Montacute by train to Axminster, and then conveying us all in a carriage and pair to a row of houses at the extreme west of the town, a row called Ozone Terrace, a name that never failed to charm and amuse my mother. Ozone Terrace was happily situated for us children. We soon discovered that these houses stood close to 'The Landslide', a wild 'forest' far more interesting to us than was the Cobb even with its harbour and customs house. This undercliff – rough, rocky, and luxuriant – extends westward almost as far as Seaton. For centuries the coastline must have been disordered here, but the natural chaos of its outline was accentuated beyond imagination in the year 1840, when no less than fifty acres of good farmland slid down.

We used to call this borderland to Lyme Regis 'the Fairy Glade' – and no wonder! It included a hundred dells with secret silent lawns surrounded by rankest undergrowth. In such places Ariel, that 'tricksie sprite', might have been set to serve the term of his second punishment, crying out 'as fast as mill-wheels strike', pegged tight, as Prospero had threatened, in the 'knotty entrails' of an oak. Nor would anyone be surprised to come upon Miranda and Caliban standing close, the tender girl out of a pure benevolence trying to teach the blinking eyes of the hairy monster to distinguish a man, a dog, and a lantern in the shadows of the harvest moon. Sir George Somers, who was wrecked on the 'still-vexed Bermoothes', and from the tales of whose adventures many of the ideas of *The Tempest* are derived, was himself born at Lyme Regis. I have never been to Bermuda, but I have seen certain coastlines in the West Indies that in their physical features resemble closely 'The Landslide' of Lyme Regis, though the flora, of course, is entirely different. In the spring the hawthorn-trees of this Dorset wilderness can hardly be matched anywhere else in England, acres upon acres of embossed and garlanded May flowers, their rich smell, redolent of a careless happy sensuality, for a few fugitive days making the surrounding air heavy with delight – so soon, soon, lost in the noiseless scattering of a myriad unnoticed petals, white and round.

At one time during the Great War it was the occupation of my brother Willie to collect cattle in the Congo and trek them down to depots of the British troops then serving in German East Africa. Besides the natives he had one white man with him, a Dorset man whose employment it had been in the fat days of peace to drive 'holiday fools' to and fro between Axminster and Lyme Regis. During the long equatorial nights my brother would often read out of his copy of William Barnes's poems, so that both he and his companion might be reminded of their homes; and sometimes this 'jolly postboy' would while away the time by describing to my brother the exact habits of a great grey gelding which throughout the 'nineties had munched oats, damp and dry, in the stables of the *Black Dog*; or sometimes by recounting to him stories of after-noons spent with buxom nursemaids tumbling in the bracken of the Fairy Glade at that time of the year when the white flowers of the privet had turned rusty red, and the lower bells of the foxgloves were already lost, and late summer flies were everywhere murmuring in the patched sunshine. Then with their heads full of old Dorset memories they would lie side by side until waked by the punctual crowing of my brother's farmyard cock, his heart's delight, which he carried along with him on all his journeys through forest and plain, and which on fine nights would invariably settle itself to roost on the spear of the tent-pole as though trying to simulate the brass vane on the top of St Catherine's Church at Montacute.

Lyme Regis at one time was a great place for fishing, but now, save for a little 'potting', few men go out. From White Nose on any day when the visibility was average I used to be able to see beyond Lyme Regis to the chalk cliffs of Beer, and it is from this Devonshire village, and from Sidmouth still further to the west, that most of the fishing in this quarter of the Bay is done. The Sidmouth fishermen and the Lympstone men, or 'stumpy-tail hookers' as they are nicknamed, often take their 'marks' from Rousdon – that is to say, locate their exact position on a fishing bed by getting this far-seen landmark above 'The Landslide' of Lyme Regis in exact line with some nearer 'sight'. 'Thousand-in-Bush and Rousdon,' Bob Wooley might shout across the waves to Tom. It is an odd fact that many of these 'marks' that are every day upon the lips of the fishing brotherhood would mean nothing to the landsman if he heard them alluded to in conversation. A particularly conspicuous field from the sea may earn itself a name such as 'Thousand-in-Bush' and perhaps be known as 'honey-plot' by the labourer who for more than half a century has been turning over its tilth at the plough's tail.

The occupations of the inhabitants of Lyme have been various. In the year 774 Cenwulf granted land to certain men whose office it became to boil salt out of sea-water for use in the butteries and kitchens of Sherborne Abbey. In Queen Elizabeth's days the shipping that sheltered in the lea of the Cobb was, it is said, 'one-sixth that of London'. Later the manufacture of serge cloth flourished here. When I was a boy there were lime-kilns on the shore beyond Ozone Terrace. New fashions, new houses, have largely marred the simple dignity of this old Dorset town; only the Cobb has been found firm to resist every change, still obstinately fulfilling the primitive task for which it was built.

Montacute House

IN the year 1931, Montacute House, one of the most perfect examples of an Elizabethan country house in England, was formally taken over by the National Trust and so became a State monument safe from mutilation or destruction. It had been the home of the Phelips family for three hundred and fifty years. A Phelips had built it and a Phelips had sold it. Montacute House is entirely constructed of Ham Hill stone, a golden habitation speaking elegantly enough of the prosperity of the Tudor times, when, under the rule of a headstrong dynasty, a moiety of peace was ensured throughout the land of England, and noblemen and gentry came no longer to consider entrenched and moated castles necessary for their safety.

It was in the year 1886 that my father was offered the living of Montacute by Mr W. R. Phelips, and when I was two years old we moved from Dorchester to our new home, a large Victorian vicarage.

It was my privilege therefore to witness at close quarters the last years of this Reformation family in their celebrated dwelling. When I recall my childhood I often now feel as if I had lived two lives, one in the eighteenth century and one in the twentieth. Overlooking the moss-grown wall of the rook-haunted, garlic-floored spinney down by the old Montacute Mill I well remember in our nursery walks seeing a notice-board with the words 'Beware of Man Traps' still clearly legible upon its weather-worn wood.

It has been for three generations the business of my family as country clergymen to stand between the landed gentry and the people of the village. This was an office my father was called upon to perform at Montacute. The Squire was a highly cultured gentleman with a kindly disposition, but the traditions of his class were firmly fixed in him. He never questioned his right to be an autocratic ruler over the lives of all those who lived upon his hereditary acres, and the democratic assertiveness that became common among the working classes toward the latter end of the nineteenth century was constantly resented by him.

In those days there were beggar women to be found in almost every parish. Nancy Cooper, an old witch woman, would come from her hovel in 'the hungry air of Odcombe' to gather sticks in the Montacute Park. The Squire never interfered with the activities of this aged woman. Perhaps he regarded her as part of his feudal estate, like some twisted tree that he would by no means let his woodsman tamper with.

Her daughter Betsy, whose birth had been the cause of her disgrace, was the old beggar woman's constant companion, and now grown to middle life was little less tattered than was her mother.

This Betsy I came to know well. Once when my brother John and I met her in the Odcombe Street we tried to get her to show us where her mother was buried. She went pathetically stumbling to and fro over the graves with tears rolling down her cheeks, repeating again and again, 'I be so mazed, I be, I didn't mind now where she do lie – she were a blessed mother and no mistake. 'Tis the nights when I do miss she terrible bad – the rats out on boards.'

The Squire's mother must have been about the same age as Nancy

Cooper, and yet how different had been the life of this other human female of high rank!

I do not think I have ever seen an old lady with so delicate a complexion. Even in her great age the poise of her head was light and graceful as a rose upon its stalk. The moulding of her skull was as fragile as that of the most precious porcelain and there was a flush upon her cheeks that reminded me of the inside of some of the sea shells in my father's cabinet. Her head was as ethereal in appearance as was Shelley's head, and she was, as a matter of fact, the daughter of Shelley's cousin, and the poet's first love, the same who forsook him to bestow the favours of her beauty upon the wealthy Squire of Coker Court in Somerset.

When old Nancy and her daughter would, with crooked spines, be 'sticking' under the great Montacute sycamores, crooning to each other on the eternal subjects of back and belly, this little light-footed great lady could be seen walking along the drive that ran under the avenue to Galpin's Lodge; unless she had chosen, as she sometimes did, the damp woodland path of Park Cover, a woodland path bordered by a shelving bank thick with mosses out of which in the autumn slippery toadstools of bright scarlet would grow. Who ever knew the long, long thoughts that were revolving in that solitary old woman's head, so aristocratic and so ancient, as she trod the ancestral woods of her husband's family, which, during those mild wet months before Christmas, never ceased from their melancholy dripping?

Her husband, the Squire's father, inherited eighteenth-century tastes, and through his love of gaming had so compromised the

Phelips estate that it never afterwards recovered. In the hall there is an oil painting of him standing life-size in his park, tall hat in hand, the great house he ruined reduced by perspective to the size of a doll's house.

Near Ilchester there are two farms called Sock and Beerly. These farms at one time rounded off the Phelips property to the north. I used to be told by the country people this story about them. The gambling Squire was staying at Weymouth, and on a wet afternoon, having nothing to do, staked a bet on one of two flies that were crawling up the window-pane. When his friend's fly reached the wooden plinth which marked the winning post of this fantastic circus race, the idle sparks who were watching heard the Master of Montacute mysteriously exclaim, 'There go Sock and Beerly.'

One of my earliest recollections of Mrs Phelips, senior, is of her driving me and her grandson Gerard, who was my own age, to Yeovil. Arrived in the town, she told the coachman to draw up at the toy-shop which stood opposite *The Choughs*. On the proprietor's obsequiously hurrying out to the carriage door, he was instructed to give us our choice of all his wares. I was so bewildered as I was ushered round the crowded passages of the small shop that I selected a painted tricycle that went by clockwork, afterward envying the cooler judgement of my companion, who brought back for our inspection in the gallery a very expensive, and apparently inexhaustible, conjuring box.

Often we would be invited to a nursery tea with the four Phelips children. We would walk down the long drive on those winter afternoons with our black shining house shoes in a basket, and

Miss Beales sedately leading the way. I remember choking at one of those teas and being carried behind the heavy winter curtains so that I might recover from my embarrassment in private, and how, before making my appearance once more at the candle-lighted tea table, I climbed up on the sill to look out of the high window and was amazed to find that in the courtyard below all was as bright as day. In that one glimpse through the small glass panes I received an impression of the enchantment of moonshine that has remained with me all my life – the fountain, the dovecot, the stone flags, the very weeds in their crevices edged with an exact hoarfrost whiteness.

It was Marjorie, the elder of the two Phelips girls, who had put me behind the curtain. She had always protected me since, under my brother John's direction, we had acted *Macbeth* and I had played the part of her little son, the son of Lady Macduff, piping out to her the words 'As birds do, mother.' The Squire, I remember, invented a method of imitating the sound of thunder by beating a large sheet of tin with a broom handle, and was amused because, for reasons of temperance, my mother would not agree to having wine served to us at the banquet, but in its stead gave us raspberry vinegar.

The interior of Montacute House stirred my imagination – the armory for example, with helmets and cuirasses used at the time of the Great Rebellion. Whenever I passed through this high square-shaped room I experienced a kind of *Ivanhoe* romance, and although the Phelips family came into prominence after the Wars of the Roses, echoes from the days of medieval chivalry would be clearly audible to me as I looked up at the weapon-hung walls of the civil ante-chamber. The main stairway was exciting also, the long stone slabs worn uneven by so much Phelips shoe leather; but most wonderful of all it was to step suddenly into the immense gallery that stretched one hundred and eighty feet from end to end of the house.

How the lonely memories of the old gallery would be scattered, as, with the careless voices of living children, we burst in upon its emptiness; and how hollow, how resonant, its bare boards would sound as our quick feet went pattering, racing down them, unheedful of anything but the impinging actuality of our moment's holiday! How swiftly, too, on a rainy afternoon the time would go by in so spacious a playing room! The great rocking-horse was kept there, the highest-stepping dapple gray ever built by a carpenter, left alone through so many long hours to contemplate with painted eye the procrastinating twilights of the morning and evening shading their way through sixteen windows, along the coved ceiling of this vast Elizabethan corridor.

The rain would beat against one or other of the high oriel windows at each end of the gallery, where, to the south, the village was overlooked, or where, at the other end, the stately ornamental North Gardens could be seen, with their dark drenched yew trees standing like royal sentinels against the meadows that rose into view beyond the privileged enclosure.

How soon death – impersonal, implacable – removes the fairy-tale characters from the dreams of our lives! Where now is the old Squire, and where now the young Squire, and where the second daughter of the house, whose hair was of the finest golden texture –

the hair of a princess in a story-book, as indeed she always seemed, whether leaning from the top of one of the garden walls to pick an apricot sweetened by the summer sun, or in a wide summer hat seated at the back of one of the Pitt Pond pleasure boats?

I do not think any occurrence I have observed in my life has given me sharper understanding of the insubstantiality of all temporal values than the separation of this house from the Phelipses. How completely for centuries they had dominated the countryside of South Somerset! They sold their hereditary farms and disposed of their hereditary manor with apparent indifference. It had not ever been in their style to wear their hearts upon their sleeves, and the outer world was never permitted to gauge at what emotional cost they were finally divided from the wood and stones and pasture lands that had for so long been theirs in perpetual freehold.

As a boy I used to visit a bed-ridden Montacute labourer. He was so old that to move himself at all he had to lay hands on a rope-end tied to the bottom rail of his rusty bedstead. This old man initiated me into an odd tradition that must have been current for generations in the village. The Phelips crest represents a blazing fire held in an iron cresset, and in years gone by some inventive mind among the commonalty must have suggested the following explanation of the sign. In a far period of antiquity, even before Thomas Phelips possessed himself of 'half a burgage' in the Montacute parish, the rightful heir of the property had been burned to death. The King of England, hearing of the deed, had given orders that the Phelips family should for all times carry the flaming beacon as their sign – 'to mind 'em of it for everlasting.'

The crest is familiar to everybody who lives in Montacute, and has been so for centuries. It is placed on each side of the great gates of the west drive and is painted clear for all eyes to see on the swinging tavern board that hangs outside the *Phelips Arms* at the top of the Borough. Without doubt, the explanation of its meaning communicated to me by old John Hann on his death-bed was the one generally accepted by the apple-orchard labourers and Ham Hill quarrymen with heads besotted with cider. To this day I remember certain of the old man's more dramatic expressions. 'Thik sign on top of they girt postics along by Vicarage do tell o' sommat,' and again, 'My granfer would say, God Almighty will shift 'em for it, may be in thy time, may be in thy childer's time, but sure as day comes he'll unroosty 'em.'

I upon occasion meet a member of this family. This grand-daughter of the Squire is a tall girl and remarkably handsome, her features carrying upon them the very stamp to be observed in many of the portraits of the old-world Phelipses still left hanging in the great hall of Montacute House. The least taint of worldliness is remote from her character. Indeed, I often feel that the unassuming goodness of her nature offers a reproof to all those who are tempted to stake their interest on the advantages of social pre-eminence in a world where the possession of every commodity is untrustworthy, where the footing of even a king is precarious, and where life itself is for every man and for every woman as fugitive as is an inconsequential dream.

Ham Hill

THE importance of a hill as a landmark in a district can by no means be always measured by its elevation. Ham Hill is a good example of this. Despite its modest proportions it is an eminence remarkably conspicuous from all directions. Men harvesting in the rich arable lands of Taunton Vale look across at it. 'Drowners' employed in cutting osiers in the dykes of Sedgemoor watch its outline for weather portents. It is clearly visible from the eastern foothills of the Quantocks, and shepherds on the Mendips and Corton Beacon have from their childhood been familiar with its shape, as it were the shape of a couchant lion which for centuries has lain perfectly motionless against the horizon, the vigilant warden of the wide water-meadows of the west.

To account for the apparently inexhaustible supply of stone that the hill has always provided, the old women of Montacute used to assure my father with the utmost gravity that the stone 'grew', and when one considers the number of the abbeys, churches, manor houses, farms, cowsheds, pounds, bridges, field walls, scullery floors and milestones which once lay raw in the bowels of this yellow mountain, this belief appears almost plausible. I have often wondered out of which particular quarry of Ham Hill the stones that form the fan tracery of the roof of Sherborne Abbey were lifted – perhaps from the same bed that was destined to provide flagstones for the notorious Ilchester gaol, stones of devotion and stones of despair deriving from a single matrix of unimplicated nature!

The late Mr W. B. Wildman, the old Fifth Form master at Sherborne, whose wide Rabelaisian imagination awakened the intelligences of so long a procession of English schoolboys, enlivening the dullest lesson with a characteristic mixture of wit and learning, would often make reference to the amphitheatre at the northern end of Ham Hill, thereby bringing vividly before the minds of his pupils the period of the Roman occupation. In graphic language he would describe how some wretched subject Briton would be dragged to this diminutive arena to make a soldier's holiday, either by fighting against another of his race, or against some wild beast imported from a far distant jungle. On such occasions I would listen to his words with all the lively personal attention natural to a boy who hears allusions made to a locality familiar to his holiday life. As I grew older I would often examine the molehills around the amphitheatre, and I found the flat muscular hands of those little gentlemen in velvet were in the habit of unwittingly casting up scraps of Roman pottery in their sedulous subterranean tunnelling after earthworms. On these wide northern levels of the hill, covered so smoothly with turf, sheep find the best grazing in the county. We used to come here to discover whether the floods were out. What a sight they were after a period of heavy rain, a wide sheet of white water covering half the county, stretching away past Athelney and Bridgewater to the western sea! And how rewarding to walk on Ham Hill on a fine spring day when the fields of Longload and High Ham lie prosperously awaiting the return of another summer; when the daisy paddocks immediately below are patched with the drying amber-coloured skins of the gloving factories; when dandelions are out everywhere in the roadside hedges; and the songs of larks are so loud that they all but drown the scrannel pipings of the little Hebditch shepherd boy. Then at last the night takes possession of the hill under the widespread silence of the stars, with aromatic winds blowing gently up over the ancient vallums from the distant hayfields of Wullam's Mill. Forty years have so entirely altered the manner of our living that it has become no easy matter to envisage the life of Ham Hill as it was during the last quarter of Queen Victoria's reign, with rumbling carts bringing down skilfully moulded blocks cradled on beds of bracken, and with ill-paid men in dusty yellow-powdered breeches – in breeches of gold ('Stoke roughs', as the less generous landed gentry did not hesitate to call them) at the head of the horses, every one of them hearty Sunday night drinkers and stout voters for Strachey. What toil those Ham Hill horses, with their defeated tragic heads, used to endure hauling wagons up the steep ways in the dust of summer and the mud of winter, and then coming down again with perilously heavy loads, skid pans on wheels, but even so with the old carts dangerously jolting and liable to get out of control.

Ham Hill was always a favourite place for political demonstrations. It was here that George Mitchell, the man from the plough, Montacute born and Montacute bred, used to hold his big meetings every Whitsun Monday, hiring no less than seven brass bands to help Joe Arch in his fight for the franchise of the agricultural labourer. He would arrive in a horse-brake with his mother sitting next the driver, with a placard before her on which the words GO

ON were inscribed in large type, and another behind her with the words COME ON enormously displayed. However, in spite of all his hearty good nature and energy and sense of publicity, Mr Mitchell was never able to get himself nominated for Parliament, and at the beginning of the century he died in London in poor circumstances, a disappointed man.

The Frying Pan end of Ham Hill is the popular end, but my own preference has always been for the south-western end. This is where the spirit of the ancient hill has been least disturbed. The whole sloping section that lies between Jack O' Beards and Tinker's Spring offers a wayfarer a wonderful prospect of rural peace. It is easy to understand how the finer spirits of the neighbourhood have taken to the civilised and honourable employment of apple growing, tending their Tom Puts, Hornets, Leather Jackets, and Pippins under clouds as grey as the feathers of a wood pigeon's breast, clouds scarcely distinguishable from the blue mists that from morning to evening in the autumnal haze obscure the course of the River Parrett as it idly meanders through one fat meadow after the other of the most fertile valley in the West of England.

On the Other Side of the Quantocks

W HEN we were children, no holiday excursion gave us more happiness than a day spent on the Quantocks. These moorland hills, rising north-west from Taunton and stretching almost to the Bristol Channel, were very exciting to us. I suppose their attraction depended largely upon the nature of their scenery, which was utterly different from that of our home. We were used enough to South Somerset, with its clay and mud – 'bad for the rider, good for the bider' – whereas these wild Ishmaelitic hills possessed the charm of the unfamiliar.

The other day, after an interval of a quarter of a century, I saw them again. The occasion that impelled me this time was a sad one. I went to visit the grave of a girl who, during the cold weeks of last January, had died at the old fishing village of Watchet and had been buried there. A particular poignancy attended this death. She had left us at the New Year to look for a house in the West Country. She and her husband had found a place that suited them exactly, and were about to return to London to make the final arrangements incident to their new life, when, after an illness of only two days, she was dead.

I have been told that the Chinese emphasise a difference between ordinary partings and these other particular partings when, in our ignorance of the crooked ways of fate, we separate from those we love for ever. It is their rumour also that an approaching death will cast a forward shadow. It certainly seems to me in retrospect that when I last saw her I had had an obscure premonition of what was to happen. She was suffering from a cold, and, lying in the corner of a wide cottage bed, she looked alarmingly fragile. I remember also that there came to me, as I walked back over the downs, certain chance glimpses of her in the past, glimpses that presented themselves as distinctly as pictures. I saw her waiting beside the standing August corn, her hand shading her eyes. I saw her in the seaweed pool at the bottom of the White Nose; and again I saw her by the fireside gravely quoting to me this lilt she had learned from her mother:

> *The best bed's a feather bed,*
> *The best bed of all,*
> *The next bed is a bed*
> *Made of pea straw.*
> *The pea straw is dirty,*
> *It will dirty all your gown;*
> *But never mind the feather bed,*
> *Lay yourself down.*

Her life had not been a completely happy one. The same intensity that gave so high a quality to her writing made it hard for her to fortify herself against the thwartings and disappointments of the years. Her spirit was as vulnerable as her body, with its bones light as the bones of a bird. She always remained a child, and if she stood on highest tiptoe could never measure more than a hogweed in a hedge.

As is so often the case with the very young, the agitations of her soul would communicate themselves directly to her body, so that if you were holding her hand when she was troubled, you would feel it vibrant and trembling like a minnow freshly taken from the net.

I set out on my expedition proposing to spend my first night at Crowcombe, a small village which lies at the foot of the Quantocks, and from there, the next day, to walk over the moors to Watchet. I found the village unchanged; the old red-brick Court House of the Carew family standing just as I remembered it, and to the right of the church the same steep lane leading on to the hills.

I took a room at the *Carew Arms* and had tea before a wide old-fashioned fireplace. As I ate my meal of whortleberry jam and Devonshire cream I seemed for the first time fully to appreciate the satisfaction that Hazlitt felt on those rare occasions when he was known to the world by no nearer definition than 'the gentleman in the parlour'. After I had finished I made up my mind to climb the Quantocks that very evening in order to discover the best route for my walk the following day.

Of all the lanes in the world this Crowcombe lane charms me most. I had never gone up it before in the springtime, and in this opening period of the year the mossy track seemed more beautiful even than I had remembered. There were periwinkles out on the crumbling walls and everywhere primroses. The lane wound upward and upward under the most splendid beech trees. The enormous trunks of these trees, rising with silent might out of the bare ground, their horizontally interlacing branches lifted higher and ever higher, awoke the spirit to the worship of Nature's strength, to the worship of her patient piety. The mute boughs, still winter-bare and yet united into one harmony, were to the eye as organ music to the ear. It seemed that not one grey-white out-spreading branch had changed its form since the days of my childhood, since that dog-day morning when, as a small boy, I had followed my Aunt Dora up the steep path, trying my best with a frond of bracken to beat away the stinging flies that troubled her. I had been impatient then to reach the top of the lane, and on this spring night the same urge was upon me. Not Table Mountain, not Mount Tamalpais, not Kenya, not Mount Carmel, not Vesuvius, not one of them all had stolen the old appeal of the West Country hill.

At last I was on the summit and looking with corporeal eye at this prospect, which on so many different occasions, in places so far from Crowcombe, had been present to the inward vision of my mind. Under the bright cold sky of that April evening I could see the hills in all their glory, fold beyond fold, combe below combe, falling away to the western ocean. On the farthest horizon it was possible to make out the mountains of Wales, while in the mid-distance, set in the silver sea of the Bristol Channel, was the island of Steep Holmes standing black against the water, black against the parrot-green nursery meadows that slope down to the very shore.

Always as children we had longed to see a red deer. In vain we had searched for one, diligently exploring each grove of stunted oak trees, pushing our way through every patch of bracken that seemed dense or secluded. We had followed the mountain streams from one rocky basin to another, but on no single occasion had we disturbed hind or stag. Now after all these years my luck had changed, for as I walked through the heather stalks blackened with fire I suddenly became aware that two of these animals had risen not fifty yards away. They were so large that almost I could imagine myself back in the highlands of Africa looking at water-buck. For a moment they remained motionless, gazing at me with the concentrated attention characteristic of wild life suddenly disturbed by man, as though even in these latter days the appearance of our kind, erect and biped, still had something startling about it, something that demanded a more exact ocular investigation than an ordinary object in nature. Then in an instant they were away over the next ridge, their antlers clear-cut against the sky, moving with a succession of absolutely silent leaps, as animals in a dream, as beasts on a tapestry come miraculously to life.

I have often noticed that any particularly favoured sight of Nature's more perfect disciplines is apt to remove for a certain time those limitations of perception that use and wont so quickly impose upon us. Without warning, without reason, we find our-selves suddenly able to experience emotions roaming and marginal, to see life with the eye of Merlin. This happened to me now as I rested on a heap of dry heather halfway down the lane, at the very spot where as a boy I had lost my silver birthday watch among the whortleberries.

Night was already falling. Never had I seen the planet Venus more beautiful, never had I seen her shine with a light more firm. As I looked at her in her isolated loveliness, the heels of my boots pressing into the soft mould of the familiar earth, and with my senses enmeshed in mystery, suddenly there was the sound of church bells upon the twilight air. It was at that moment as if this Christian sound coming up from the village below belonged really and truly to another world, a world without sorrow or death, a world no longer rude, a world where love was as gentle as mill-stream flowers and as eternal as light. Up through the naked beech tree branches came the sound as from a great distance, the fitful cadence of its tintinnabulation borne, now soft, now loud, upon the restless winds of the wood.

All Christmas nights were in the sound and all New Year Eves. It tolled for the passing of the souls of all men, of all women; it chimed for the wedding processions of true lovers who for centuries have slept dreamless far under the roots of red-berried yew trees. Now it sounded dolorous as the stroke of a harbour bell giving warning of danger in the dusk of an autumn evening; now happy as a chime from the turret of a chapel, when cuckoo-flowers and kingcups are out in the water meadows, and the prince and princess at play in their garden bower.

It was as though these bell clappers were truly ancient medieval tongues telling of days out of the past; telling of antique cradles, of the enchanted web of flaxen sheets grey with age; telling of churchyards still prosperous and emerald bright, but where the strife of this naughty world has been for ever cancelled, and where the knight and his lady have been lying without lust for a period without computation, and where the rook boy elbows the goose girl and the hen wife the swineherd with ugly brown teeth. It was a music out of the past. It told of what might have been and never has been; a music of the very borderland of the wilful senses; a music of a paradise serene and glad, where impassioned phantoms wander free, their minds, their bodies, at peace at last.

When I waked the next morning it was raining. 'You are never going on to the hills today,' remarked my hostess as she brought in my breakfast. However, by the time I had reached the top of the lane the day had begun to improve.

Hidden among some trees I came upon a small hut. I knocked on its door. A rough man appeared, and I asked him which of the tracks would bring me to Watchet. He rubbed his sandy grey hair and looked suspiciously at me. He was large-boned and unkempt, and his boots were unlaced. Eventually he gave me the directions I wanted. I stood talking to him. He had lived in his small house all his life. He made a livelihood by fetching away the carcasses of the deer killed by the hounds, and distributing the venison among the farmers and village people. For the performance of this task he had a cart and a small tough pony; and he assured me that, knowing the moors as he did, and the habits of the red deer, he scarcely ever failed to be in at the death. He told me that his name was Truggins. What the correct word in the lore of venery would be to describe a man with his duties I do not know.

I now made my way along the high ridge that lies to the west of the hills, and a proud walk it is over this shoulder of the Quantocks. To the left the traveller looks down upon the lowlands that separate them from Dunkery Beacon. The ploughed fields showed the red tilth characteristic of Devonshire, and the meadows were small and regular as chess-board squares. I came upon a weather-beaten, weather-bitten thorn tree standing by itself in a place where five grassy tracks met. Judging from the size of its trunk, it must have been of a great age. It was hoar with crisp crinkled lichen, but I noticed that every twig was decorated with living buds. It was difficult to imagine this ancient hawthorn in flower, its twisted besom branches soft with the opulent sweetness of May.

What a trysting-place this tree would make! Almost certainly it had before now been used for this recurring human need, perhaps by Ruth herself before ever she had come to wander mad and was observed by William Wordsworth trifling with her toys in the brown trout streams.

That oaten pipe of hers is mute,
Or thrown away; but with a flute
Her loneliness she cheers:

This flute, made of a hemlock stalk,
At evening in his homeward walk
The Quantock woodman hears.

I, too, have passed her on the hills
Setting her little water-mills
By spouts and fountains wild –
Such small machinery as she turned
Ere she had wept, ere she had mourned,
A young and happy Child!

I came down from the Quantocks at their north-western extremity to discover that I still had several miles to walk before reaching Watchet. The hotel where Ann Reid had died was an old and attractive building. The proprietor and his wife had done all within their power to help her. I looked at these good people with gratitude, selected as they had been out of all the population of England to cherish the last hours of this girl's life. They showed me her room. It was an ordinary hotel bedroom, but I noticed that between the roofs of the houses across the street a wide space of open sky must have been visible from her pillow. It has always seemed to me no inconsequent matter what our eyes look upon in the hour of death. It was garden birds twittering in the clematis outside her window that made up my mother's last impression of earth life.

I walked to the churchyard on the hill. There was the grave under the farther wall, with the mould still showing raw and with strips of green turf laid unevenly on the mound.

The church of Watchet is dedicated to St Decuman. It stands on the summit of a hill midway between Exmoor and the Quantocks. The body of the church is hidden by trees, but its tower is visible from a great distance like a kind of Glastonbury Tor rising by itself. I was happy to know that she who had always been so steadfast a champion of the spiritually oppressed should have her burial plot marked by so brave a sign.

When all has been said, how abject a grave can look! 'We are the dead' – 'We are the dead' – 'We are the dead!' Yet out of the dumb ground there rose no word of reproach. 'Every day, every hour that you breathe you experience a miracle. You are still free and alive. Brief as a rainbow your dream also will be. There is no clemency, no reprieve, no escape; no, not for the strongest heart deep mortised in life. "A straw, a hair hath done it.'"

Exmoor

WHEN I was living at White Nose I received a letter from a small coal merchant in Dorchester offering to sell me a load of peat, and before many days I had a good stack of this excellent fuel in my backyard. It is likely that never before had peat been burned on the famous chalk headland. On late frosty after-noons, when the wind was blowing from the north, and the hare 'limp'd trembling through the frozen grass', the gipsy-like aroma of burning turf would come to me upon the fresh inland air. It was a rough incense evocative of far-away memories.

When I was fifteen years old my brother Littleton, who was ten years my senior, planned that we should spend a fortnight fly-fishing on Exmoor. He provided me with a rod, and used to stand by me for hours on the Montacute lawn teaching me how to throw a fly. Up to that time my only experience of the sport had been bottom-fishing in Pitt Pond. I would be content to sit by the edge of that large woodland tarn, angling in dark waters, my eyes fixed upon my coloured float, hoping and hoping to see it quiver and be carried, a moment afterwards, resolutely out of sight. I had never been to Exmoor before, and it was an adventure that influenced my whole life. We arrived at Minehead with the April sunshine splashing down on pavements, and with daffodils in flower in every garden. A farm-cart was at the station waiting to convey us to Malmsmead; the driver was a young man who spoke with a broad Devonshire accent, his 'twoos' sounding to my ears like a foreign language.

It was nearly five o'clock in the afternoon before we reached the top of Porlock Hill. It was one of those spring evenings that seem as cool as a grotto, when all life appears suddenly wide awake like a little girl talking to herself in her nursery cot. The landlord of the *Ship Inn* stepped brisk and gay along his narrow office-passage, now no longer darkened by doors closed against winds and sleet. Boys were out in the dewy lanes playing and calling, and the first petals of flowers were beginning to fall upon the first white dust. My mood as I rested by my brother's side on the top of Porlock Hill was one of utter happiness. Lying in the heather, I had in my mind no vision of the place to which the cart, not yet to be seen at the crest of the steep road, was about to carry us; I only was aware that the evening sky seemed wider in its circumference than I had ever known it in South Somerset, extending its celestial hoop far off over the wild enfolded hills, and far over a broad sea of speedwell-blue, emphatic of life's fortunate freedoms.

We reached the farm at twilight. While our evening meal was preparing I had time to run out and stand on the bridge to watch the trout poised in the clean water below. Day and night the sound of the river was audible in John Ridd's farm. In the afternoons when the baker called, energetic and with no time for thoughts other than those connected with his business, the unending melody continued, and when I waked in the small hours, curled up beside my brother on a huge feather bed, I would hear it still, this music utterly unfamiliar to my ears, different altogether from the regular breaking of the waves on Weymouth beach, different from the sound of the rain driving against the leaves of the trees in a summer garden.

It was as though we lay during those nights dreaming in the bowl of a huge silver bell, a bell that was always and always ringing for the festival of life, with a tune as simple and incessant as that which comes from the banded neck of a bellwether browsing amongst thyme and devil's-bit.

That first evening meal in the old farm I have never forgotten. A deep dish of Devonshire cream, and a loaf of brown bread with lightly boiled fresh eggs, were set before us on a lamp-lit, tea-laid table in a room smelling of the peat fire glowing red on the open hearth; indeed, the smell of burning peat permeated the whole room – the curtains smelt of it, the Devonshire cream tasted of it!

Perhaps it was the lack of any conspicuous success with my rod that made me persuade my brother – a born fisherman, he is always happiest on the bank of a river – to sacrifice his birthday for a walk to Dunkery Beacon. We set out up Badgery Water on a morning of sunshine, our pockets stuffed with provisions. Side by side we walked over wide stretches of burned heather, the charred, twisted twigs of which kept loosening the laces of my boots. In after years when I rode across land in Africa devastated by a bush fire it was always to the fells around Dunkery Beacon that my dreams would go, as, rendered stupid by the sun, I dozed in the saddle while my white Somali pony, with ever-blackening fetlocks, made his way over the vast waste.

At certain seasons we often hear the piping of curlews as they fly across Chaldon Down on their way to the seashore, but it was on this April walk across Exmoor that for the first time I listened to their wild voices. We had sat down on some tussocks at the foot of Dunkery Beacon and must have disturbed one of the birds, for round and round us it flew, often near enough for its long curved bill to be clearly visible. In nature if any sound is burdened with romance it is the curlew's call. Don Quixote on two separate occasions explained to Sancho Panza how King Arthur at his death was transformed into a crow, and truly, when we hear the dolorous crying of a curlew far up in the heavens, it is not difficult to imagine that we are listening to the bird spirit of a king wailing for the fair dust of a paramour dead long centuries ago.

From Dunkery Beacon we dropped down through the Horner Woods, and it was then to my great delight that we saw red deer. That civil people can still be found willing to hunt to death these proud beasts is to me extraordinary. It is indeed a striking example of how the sanctions of the unimaginative conventional world can obscure, even for intelligent people, the higher values of life. Who can say whether a warrantable stag is less sensitive or less highly developed than a stabled horse? Even Thomas Bewick, always rough and ready, noticed their eyes as being 'peculiarly beautiful, soft, and sparkling'. Surely the laughing girls who every August gather at Cloutsham Farm to kill so god-like an animal, as it were for a game, must have hidden their hearts at the breaking of the cold summer's dawn in the grey water of Watchet or Bridgewater Bay!

All that is deathless of me I have laid
In a crystal box on the magic sea,
With the currents of stars and the winds of space
It is drifting away in eternity.

Let us dismiss from our minds such sorrowful controversies and return to the cliffs of Dorset, where even the foxes 'wise in counsel' are left unmolested. Often at White Nose I have lain flat upon a fresh-ploughed furrow in order that I might smell the very body of the earth, and on those occasions when the seaside air carried upon its gusts the tang of my peat fire it would seem to me that I was inhaling also the earth's light breath. Through the mysterious power of such simple sacramental experiences it becomes more easy in old age, or in sickness, for a lover of life to borrow with resignation the octogenarian's apostrophe to the earth in the *Canterbury Tales*:

> *I knokke with my staf erly and late.*
> *And saye 'Deare Moder let me in'.*

Dartmoor

POETICAL as are the Quantock Hills, exciting to the spirit as Exmoor is, neither of these West Country ranges can be compared to Dartmoor Forest, that vast tract of waste land, so stern in character, which to the extent of an area of two hundred square miles sprawls itself over Devonshire. If the Quantocks suggest what is lyrical in literature and Exmoor a ballad quality, Dartmoor may be said to affect us as some grave passage from the Scriptures, a passage designed by the men of the old time to bring home to the apprehension the impermanence of mortal life.

A few days spent on the moors, and we grow accustomed to such a habit of thought. However brightly the sun may shine, however high the clouds may float across the heavens, however much the tumbling streams may glisten and sparkle, or the rowan trees delight the eye with their windless shivering, it is impossible to be in the forest for any length of time without giving heed to this solemn and insistent homily. It is as if the Tors themselves, those granite monuments of obdurate matter, were visible tokens carved out of eternity. For how perdurable these huge heaps of boulders can look – High Willhays, Haytor, Yes Tor – each one of them a doomsday temple under the sun, offering shelter and sanctuary to the prick-eared fox and a resting place for the sentinel buzzard.

Before these uncouth altars celebrating the astral rift of the earth's birth the lives of bird, animal, and fish appear but as shadows of the homeless winds. Like somnolent saurians of prodigious girth the long, grey rocks lie one upon another as in the tropics I have

137

seen crocodiles do, flat head to dragon tail, dragon tail to flat head. Before such indestructible masses of petrifaction the spine of a trout, so slim and pliable in its shade of quick flesh, seems how light! The contrived body of a restless bird, how fleeting! And our own bones, with their supple kneecaps, their crab-pot ribs, their hollow skulls, as akin to dust, and as frangible, as beakers of clay.

There is a celebrated line in Homer which can be translated: 'Like to the race of leaves the race of man is.' On a Dartmoor gravestone I read these words: 'We be as leaves' – words showing that in the eighteenth century the thought of the men of the moor was not very different from the thought of the men of the Isles of Greece three thousand years ago. Yet how glad on a May morning Steeperton can look, with her twin mountain rivers crossing their waters over the rocks in diminutive falls of dazzling spray, or gathering them into their deep pools where in amber, far below, the trout remain poised with heads pointing upstream. If you follow either of these streams to the watershed near Cranmere Pool, you will be well recompensed. Whenever Confucius sat by running water his disciples noticed that he would before long fall to weeping. They tried to discover why this was so, and eventually surmised that the movement of the water put him in mind of the flowing away of all earth life – the old man with skin apple-wrinkled from the sun, and the child with its toy, the one scarcely more lasting than the other.

To invalidate the cruder rewards of the senses, the idealists play with the contention that without mind there exists no incontestable objective reality. On these Dartmoor river banks, with sight, sound, smell, touch, and taste uniting their testimony, such sophistries are easily discounted. I looked into a recess between two rocks where a piece of suspended moss, drenched and enduring, was being thrown backward and forward by the cold rushing torrent. My consciousness was the sole witness of this event, of this actual physical happening in an apex of time, and my perceptive identity was envisaging the significant form of a parcel of atoms that made up an absolute reality. Doubt not, this chilled scrap of herbage would have been tossing, so and not otherwise, had I never happened to rest where I chanced to see it. Apart from my intelligence it had its own terrifying existence. However far into the firmament I flung my mind, to the moon's frozen escarpments or to the margins of our island universe, this morsel of moss would still preserve its same condition of positive being.

As I looked up from meditating upon the verity of inhuman poetry as manifested by so puny a tassel I saw upon a rock not twenty yards away a ring ousel; lightly it flew upstream, dancing over the drab boulders with its distinguishing white collar easily visible in the sunlight. Presently I approached the wildest part of the moor, with bogs and mires in every direction, a kind of Siberian tundra, and it was just here that there was carried to me over the tufted heather, over the bog cotton, the clear incorrigible call of a cuckoo. With all the meadows of Devonshire to choose from, I was amazed that this bird should have penetrated to such a wilderness. How could it have deserted for so barren a waste the leafy lane behind the Oxenham Manor, behind that ancient dwelling-house which, for all that it solidly stands in South Tawton, so strangely suggests to a traveller a French chateau, and remains today very much as it was in Elizabethan times when a son of the house left its home pastures to go to the Spanish Main and to be hung at Lima? What was this feckless fowl with open beak and cocked fantail doing on these high dun-coloured platforms tumbling after 'his aunts' in a wild rowan tree? Here is no canton for this careless opponent of duty and domesticity, for this free bird whose native habitat is a flaming swamp in the Congo or the Cameroons. I also heard the lark everywhere. Above the dry grass, above the dry open soil, above the boulders, the air was quivering with the ecstatic music of this possessed spirit, heedless of everything but the joy of being alive, formed out of dust into a crested handful of buoyant feathers, with its mate, its dusky darling, hidden below, her breast pressed to the peat.

Some thirty or forty years since, Scotch sheep were brought to Dartmoor. It was thought that with their long fleeces they would be able to withstand better than the original close-wooled Dartmoor breed the cold mists of the winter. I have never seen a true Dartmoor sheep, but the Scotch sheep are now everywhere, with their black faces peering at you like devils from behind rocks; till a moment later they run off with their long kempy mantles, which reach almost to their hoofs, jerking up and down. Tom Coryat declared that it was a custom with the Venetian nobility for anyone who lived wildly to be buried in the habiliments of a monk, so that when the last trump sounded he could make shift in such a disguise to pass himself off as one of the religious. These sheep reminded me of this hearsay, as though so many quadruped demons were playing domino in pontifical wool-white copes.

At the mere sight of my figure in the distance the Dartmoor ponies cantered away. It is sad to think that every year some of them, valued for their toughness and smallness of size, are sold to coal owners to be used for hauling in the pits. I can hardly imagine a more abrupt change of environment for one of these animals. Enjoying the freedom of a wild creature, accepting the fair weather with frolic, and enduring foul weather by turning its hindquarters to the drifting wet; at night couchant in the heather, audibly breathing with hard hoofs tucked under sensible abdomen in the stillness of starshine – and then to be suddenly roughly haltered by a man smelling of sweat, and transported along pitchy tunnels to the earth's depths, never to feel the sun's warmth penetrating its hide again, to remain buried underground, dragging, dragging, dragging out its life long after it has become blind, released only on some scarce noticed afternoon when the worn out carcass of a dead pit pony awaits the arrival of the knacker's lorry at the pit's head! Surely to a Dartmoor pony arbitrary man must appear like a monster, whether in the turmoil of Tavistock Fair, or in the gnome-lit stable where he fills blackened mangers with bottles of scant and dusty hay from the day-time world.

It is curious that no remains of palaeolithic man have ever been found on Dartmoor. It was the later neolithic peoples, the men of the Bronze Age, who set up cromlechs and stone circles upon the rough plains projecting against the skyline like jagged teeth. How these enormous stones span the long centuries, beacon signals of intelligence out of a far distant past! The conception of a perfect circle, of a mystical circumference which from the earliest times, because of its apple-like, moon-like, sun-like form, has fascinated man's imagination, was brought, it is rumoured, to Dartmoor out of Egypt, a religious legacy from those days when man first stood wondering, upright upon his feet.

Below Cawsand Beacon, near the head of a wide swamp on the margin of the moor, I came upon an alignment of stones, once placed in order, I suppose, for ceremonial purposes. They stand in three ranks and seem arranged to impart a certain prominence, perhaps for sacrificial reasons, to a large monolith. It was here that I left the moor, climbing down to a number of those walled-in plots of cultivated ground that, belonging to 'venville' crofters, mark, on every side of Dartmoor, man's pertinacious encroachments upon the obstinate heath. I soon became aware of a primitive sound peculiar to man. I have heard it in the heart of Africa and near a camp of Red Indians in the Rocky Mountains – the sound of iron striking upon stone! I looked over the wall, and in the small field saw an old labourer breaking up a protruding rock, using for his purpose a peculiar hatchet-shaped hammer. I spoke to him, asking him about the rows of stones under the Beacon.

'I have been told,' he said, 'that they stones be graveyard stones.'

'But what kind of men would ever choose to be buried in such a place?' I asked.

'Folk such as you be, and folk such as I be.'

This unanticipated turn to the conversation roused my curiosity about the stone-breaker's beliefs, and I found him to be a devout Quaker. It was to him I owed my discovery of the Quaker grave-yard at Sticklepath. I reached it by a narrow lane that leaves the main street of the village behind the great water-wheel of the mill. I do not think I have ever seen a graveyard I like better. Under a tall elder hedge was a high stone on which was carved these words:

PHIL. iv. 3. WHOSE NAMES ARE IN THE BOOK OF LIFE. In this consecrated ground are interred the bodies of the pious Quakers late residents in this village who in the year 1745 and after welcomed and entertained the Wesleys and others as they journeyed to preach the gospel through the West.

Be not forgetful to entertain strangers. HEB. xiii. 2.

Wherever I looked in this small enclosure, hardly larger than an ass's paddock, I was aware of a certain homely style that seemed natural to these Quakers, as if their spiritual sincerities and spiritual simplicities had admitted them to an understanding of the more ancient pieties. Because their feeling was sound, a certain dignity of utterance had become native to them. On one stone I read, 'Her happy spirit fled from earth to heaven', and there was another to the memory of a boy 'whom God's finger touched and he slept June 12th.' I was especially charmed by the discovery of an arbour embowered by honeysuckle. It was just such a summerhouse as Christian was resting in when he lost his Roll. It must have been put up, I think, sometime at the end of the eighteenth century. Inside there was a white wooden circular seat where five or six mourners could rest and meditate upon the uncertainty of human life – the span of days of an octogenarian Quaker, in such a place, seeming to be contracted to the duration of a summer's morning.

The walls of this delightful garden house were adorned with three scrolls. Two of these scrolls had suitable passages from the Scriptures written upon them. The third and central one presented a poem by Montgomery. The poet's name was not unfamiliar to me. It was a habit with my father to distinguish Sundays from weekdays by reading a hymn before family prayers, and as I would sit watching butterflies passing in zigzag flights over the flower beds outside the window I would often hear this name gravely pronounced with the closing of the book; for, although my father in a general way remained unimpressed by literary achievements, he always seemed concerned that these hymn poets should receive their due of honourable fame.

Even in those days I did not think Montgomery's gentle talent was of much importance to English literature. Yet with the sound of the mill stream in my ears, with green-enfolded trees sheltering the place on every side, with an old-fashioned rose at the arbour door, I could imagine no poem more fitting to the mood of that afternoon – a gentle vesper music, utterly innocent, to end so happy a day.

> *A scene sequestered from the haunts of men,*
> *The loveliest nook of all that lovely glen,*
> *Where weary pilgrims found their last repose –*
> *The High, the Low, the Mighty, and the Fair,*
> *Equal in death, were undistinguished there ...*
> *And oft the living, by affection led,*
> *Were wont to walk in spirit with their dead.*

Major Works of Llewelyn Powys

Ebony and Ivory (1923)

Thirteen Worthies (1923)

Black Laughter (1924)

Skin for Skin (1925)

The Verdict of Bridlegoose (1926)

Henry Hudson (1927)

The Cradle of God (1929)

The Pathetic Fallacy (1930)

Apples Be Ripe (1930)

A Pagan's Pilgrimage (1931)

Impassioned Clay (1931)

Glory of Life (1934)

Earth Memories (1934)

Damnable Opinions (1935)

Dorset Essays (1935)

The Twelve Months (1936)

Rats in the Sacristy (1937)

Somerset Essays (1937)

Love and Death (1939)

A Baker's Dozen (1939)

Swiss Essays (1947)

The most recent Llewelyn Powys publications have been *Wessex Memories* (2003), a collection of country essays edited by Peter J. Foss, and the same author's *Bibliography of Llewelyn Powys* (2007).

Also available from The Sundial Press

THE BLACKTHORN WINTER by PHILIPPA POWYS

The Blackthorn Winter is an ardent and uncompromising portrayal of life in rural England in the 1920s, and of one woman's battle with her own emotions. Originally published in 1930 and now reissued for the first time, it is a work that fully mirrors the free spirit and passionate nature of its author.

'A sense of immediacy informs *The Blackthorn Winter* ... The prose swerves from the abrupt to the naive; it is full of inversions, as though the author were quite unaware of the kind of language employed by her literary contemporaries. But she is not writing for a conventional novel-reading public ... The book is alive with textures and smells; it is not written about country life but out of direct experience of it, the kind of life a rural readership would recognise.' – *From the Introduction by Glen Cavaliero*

REVIEWS

'There is a distinctive energy and wildness to this work; its scenes of the harsh and peripatetic Gypsy life of the period are compelling and memorable.' – *The Times Literary Supplement*

'The charm of the book lies in its atmosphere – a heavy, slow, earthy atmosphere – and in the power of the author to conjure up country sounds and scents and scenes to such an extent that we almost cease to be readers and become participants in the story.' – *Spectator*

'Like her brother, John Cowper, Philippa Powys has a great sense of drama. Her plot is dramatically simple, her dialogue spare, and the visual beauty of *The Blackthorn Winter* has a cinematic quality ... The story of Nancy Mead is told proudly, directly, classically, and the teller offers no verdicts.' – *The Powys Society Newsletter*

HESTER CRADDOCK by ALYSE GREGORY

Hester Craddock and her sister live with their aloof brother in a cottage on a remote headland. The comfortable monotony of their routine lives is broken irrevocably by the arrival in the local village of a writer and his attractive artist friend. Casual acquaintance leads to deeper involvement as the protagonists become entangled in a web of shifting relationships, in which the desire for knowledge and experience unleashes the forces of jealousy, suspicion, and despair, with unforeseen consequences.

'Gregory's novels, so far forgotten and ignored, merit their place in the canon of modernist literature in English as exemplary studies of the human consciousness struggling to make sense of itself.' – *From the Introduction by Barbara Ozieblo*

REVIEWS

'This attractive reissue of her third novel, *Hester Craddock*, an acutely observed psychological drama, is especially welcome.' – *The Times Literary Supplement*

'*Hester Craddock* is a rich and powerful book... It is a novel of psychic moods, inner tensions and forces. However much of Alyse's personal experiences and torments went into the writing of this novel, they have been through the crucible of her imagination to produce a work of fiction of wide scale and deep intensity.' – *Rosemary Manning*

'In *Hester Craddock* ... the writing is so good that it is not necessary that it should be flawless.' – *Marianne Moore*